CADERNO DE REVISÃO

ENSINO MÉDIO
INGLÊS

Gisele Aga
Licenciada em Letras pelas Faculdades Metropolitanas Unidas (FMU). Autora de livros didáticos de Língua Inglesa para os anos finais do Ensino Fundamental, autora de materiais didáticos para programas bilíngues, editora de conteúdos didáticos, professora de Língua Inglesa para o Ensino Médio na rede particular de ensino e professora de Língua Inglesa em cursos de idiomas.

Adriana Saporito
Licenciada em Letras, com habilitação em Tradutor e Intérprete – Português e Inglês – pela Faculdade Ibero-Americana de Letras e Ciências Humanas. Professora de Literatura Brasileira, Língua Portuguesa e Língua Inglesa da rede particular de ensino, autora de livros de Língua Inglesa para Ensino Fundamental e Educação para Jovens e Adultos (EJA), editora de conteúdos didáticos.

Carla Maurício
Bacharel e licenciada em Letras pela Universidade Federal do Rio de Janeiro (UFRJ). Professora de Língua Inglesa da rede particular de ensino, editora de conteúdos didáticos, autora de livros de Língua Inglesa para os anos finais do Ensino Fundamental e do Ensino Médio.

1ª edição
São Paulo – 2016

© Editora do Brasil S.A., 2016
Todos os direitos reservados

Direção geral: Vicente Tortamano Avanso
Direção adjunta: Maria Lúcia Kerr Cavalcante Queiroz

Direção editorial: Cibele Mendes Curto Santos
Gerência editorial: Felipe Ramos Poletti
Supervisão editorial: Erika Caldin
Supervisão de arte, editoração e produção digital: Adelaide Carolina Cerutti
Supervisão de direitos autorais: Marilisa Bertolone Mendes
Supervisão de controle de processos editoriais: Marta Dias Portero
Supervisão de revisão: Dora Helena Feres
Consultoria de iconografia: Tempo Composto Col. de Dados Ltda.
Licenciamentos de textos: Cinthya Utiyama, Jennifer Xavier, Paula Harue Tozaki, Renata Garbellini
Coordenação de produção CPE: Leila P. Jungstedt

Concepção, desenvolvimento e produção: Triolet Editorial e Mídias Digitais
Diretora executiva: Angélica Pizzutto Pozzani
Diretor de operações: João Gameiro
Gerente editorial: Denise Pizzutto
Editor de texto: Camilo Adorno
Assistente editorial: Tatiana Pedroso
Preparação e revisão: Amanda Andrade, Carol Gama, Érika Finati, Flávia Venezio, Flávio Frasqueti, Gabriela Damico, Juliana Simões, Leandra Trindade, Mayra Terin, Patrícia Rocco, Regina Elisabete Barbosa, Sirlei Pinochia
Projeto gráfico: Triolet Editorial/Arte
Editora de arte: Ana Onofri, Paula Belluomini
Assistentes de arte: Beatriz Landiosi (estag.), Lucas Boniceli (estag.)
Iconografia: Pamela Rosa (coord.), Clarice França
Fonografia: Maximal Estúdio
Tratamento de imagens: Fusion DG
Capa: Paula Belluomini

Dados Internacionais de Catalogação na Publicação (CIP)
(Câmara Brasileira do Livro, SP, Brasil)

Caderno de revisão, 3º ano : your turn : ensino médio / Gisele Aga, Adriana Saporito, Carla Maurício. – 1. ed. – São Paulo : Editora do Brasil, 2016. – (Série Brasil : ensino médio)

Componente curricular: Língua estrangeira moderna – Inglês
ISBN 978-85-10-06165-0 (aluno)
ISBN 978-85-10-06166-7 (professor)

1. Inglês (Ensino médio) I. Saporito, Adriana.
II. Maurício, Carla. III. Título. IV. Série.

16-05851   CDD-420.7

Índice para catálogo sistemático:
1. Inglês : Ensino médio   420.7

Todos os esforços foram feitos no sentido de localizar e contatar os detentores dos direitos das músicas reproduzidas no CD que integra a coleção *Your Turn*. Mediante manifestação dos interessados, a Editora do Brasil terá prazer em providenciar eventuais regularizações.

Reprodução proibida. Art. 184 do Código Penal e Lei n. 9.610 de 19 de fevereiro de 1998.
Todos os direitos reservados

2016
Impresso no Brasil

1ª edição / 1ª impressão, 2016
Impresso na Arvato Bertelsmann

Rua Conselheiro Nébias, 887 – São Paulo/SP – CEP 01203-001
Fone: (11) 3226-0211 – Fax: (11) 3222-5583
www.editoradobrasil.com.br

APRESENTAÇÃO

Caro aluno,

Apresentamos o Caderno de revisão de nossa coleção. Ele foi concebido com a finalidade de instrumentalizá-lo para que revise e amplie seu conhecimento da língua inglesa visando a preparação para o Enem e vestibulares. Para tal, este caderno oferece revisões de aspectos linguísticos e estratégias de aprendizagem e uso da língua inglesa, bem como atividades planejadas com base no modelo do Enem e outras autênticas, extraídas de vestibulares de todas as regiões do Brasil.

Ao trabalhar com este caderno, você terá a oportunidade de revisar conteúdos e colocá-los em prática por meio da leitura de textos e de atividades de múltipla escolha ou discursivas, que cobrem as principais habilidades exigidas nos exames de encerramento do Ensino Médio: identificar aspectos culturais e sociais, buscar compreensão geral e detalhada, estabelecer relações entre textos em língua inglesa com as estruturas linguísticas, sua função e seus usos sociais, bem como associar vocábulos e expressões de tais textos aos seus temas.

Nós, autoras, estamos certas de que você encontrará neste material mais uma fonte de construção de conhecimento aliada ao trabalho enriquecedor desenvolvido ao longo da coleção.

Bom trabalho!

As autoras

Sumário

Language Review 6
Learning Strategies 11
Simulados Enem 14
Vestibulares 21
Gabarito 59

LANGUAGE REVIEW

Subject and Object Pronouns

▶ *Subject Pronouns* (pronomes pessoais do caso reto) são usados para evitar a repetição dos sujeitos nas orações.

▶ *Object Pronouns* (pronomes pessoais do caso oblíquo) são usados para substituir os objetos das orações.

	Subject Pronouns	Object Pronouns
Singular	I	Me
Singular	You	You
Singular	He	Him
Singular	She	Her
Singular	It	It
Plural	We	Us
Plural	You	You
Plural	They	Them

Relative Pronouns

Relative Pronouns (pronomes relativos) são usados quando queremos acrescentar informações sobre uma pessoa, coisa, lugar etc. mencionado anteriormente.

O pronome relativo *who* é usado quando nos referirmos a pessoas.

Which é empregado para coisas, animais e ideias.

That substitui *who* e *which* na maioria dos casos, porém é mais informal do que ambos.

Where é usado para lugares e *when* para referências de tempo.

Whose é usado quando queremos nos referir a quem pertence alguma coisa.

Reflexive Pronouns

Reflexive Pronouns (pronomes reflexivos) são usados quando o sujeito e o objeto da oração são iguais, quando queremos enfatizar o agente de uma ação, ou quando temos o sentido de sozinho(a), sozinhos(as), sem ajuda, precedidos pela preposição *by*.

	Subject Pronouns	Reflexive Pronouns
Singular	I	Myself
Singular	You	Yourself
Singular	He	Himself
Singular	She	Herself
Singular	It	Itself
Plural	We	Ourselves
Plural	You	Yourselves
Plural	They	Themselves

Wh- Question Words

Wh- Question Words (pronomes interrogativos) são usados para fazermos perguntas.

Pronomes interrogativos	Para perguntar sobre
How	modos ou maneiras
How big	tamanhos
How many	quantidades
How much	quantidade ou preços
How often	frequência
How old	idades
What	ações, coisas
When	tempo
Where	lugares
Which	elementos específicos
Who	pessoas
Whose	posses
Why	razões

Caderno de revisão

Genitive Case

O *Genitive Case* (caso genitivo ou possessivo) expressa posse entre dois substantivos, podendo referir-se a pessoas ou animais. É formado pelo acréscimo do apóstrofo + s ('s) ao substantivo.

Após substantivos no plural terminados em –s, acrescentamos somente o apóstrofo (').

Quando há mais de um possuidor e queremos indicar posse comum, inserimos 's após o nome do último possuidor; mas quando queremos indicar posse individual, inserimos 's após cada um dos possuidores.

Possessive Adjectives

Possessive Adjectives (adjetivos possessivos) são utilizados para palavras que têm a função de modificar os substantivos indicando posse. Eles são posicionados antes dos substantivos.

	Subject Pronouns	Possessive Adjectives
Singular	I	My
Singular	You	Your
Singular	He	His
Singular	She	Her
Singular	It	Its
Plural	We	Our
Plural	You	Your
Plural	They	Their

Comparatives and Superlatives

Os adjetivos podem ser flexionados nos graus comparativos e superlativos. O comparativo é usado para comparar duas coisas, pessoas, lugares ou ações e o superlativo para comparar pessoas, lugares ou ações em um grupo ao qual pertencem, quando queremos dizer que tal elemento comparado pertence ao grau mais alto em um determinado aspecto.

Para formarmos o comparativo de adjetivos de uma sílaba e de alguns adjetivos de duas sílabas, acrescentamos a terminação *-er* ao final destes e para formarmos o comparativo da maioria dos adjetivos de duas sílabas e de adjetivos com três ou mais sílabas, usamos a palavra *more* antes deles.

Para formarmos o superlativo de adjetivos de uma sílaba e de alguns adjetivos de duas sílabas, acrescentamos a terminação *-est* ao final destes. O artigo definido *the* é usado antes dos adjetivos no grau superlativo.

Para formarmos o superlativo da maioria dos adjetivos de duas sílabas e de adjetivos com três ou mais sílabas, usamos a estrutura *the most* antes deles.

Formas irregulares:

Adjectives	Comparatives	Superlatives
Good	Better	The best
Bad	Worse	The worst
Far	Farther/ Further	The farthest / The furthest

Compounds with Some, Any, and No

Some e *any* (algo /algum /alguma /alguns /algumas /algo de) podem desempenhar a função de adjetivo, quando acompanham substantivos, ou de pronome, quando substituem um substantivo. *No* desempenha a função de adjetivo e *none* (nenhum, nenhuma) de pronome. *Some*, *any*, *no* e seus respectivos derivados são usados quando nos referirmos a pessoas, lugares ou coisas que não conhecemos ou não sabemos especificar com precisão.

Some e seus derivados são usados em frases afirmativas, ofertas, pedidos ou em perguntas, quando esperamos uma resposta positiva. *Any* e seus derivados são usados em frases negativas e interrogativas, e *no* e seus derivados, assim como *none*, são empregados em frases afirmativas, conferindo a elas sentido negativo.

Os derivados terminados em *-body* (ou *-one*) e *-thing* referem-se a pessoas e coisas, respectivamente, e os derivados terminados em *-where* referem-se a lugares.

-Ing endings as Nouns, Verbs, and Adjectives

Em inglês as palavras terminadas com o sufixo *-ing* não se referem somente ao *Present Continuous* ao qual geralmente são associadas. Palavras terminadas em *-ing* podem desempenhar várias funções, dentre elas as de substantivos, verbos e adjetivos.

Modal Verbs

Modal Verbs (modais) são auxiliares que conferem um significado específico aos verbos principais que os acompanham. Eles são usados na forma base e posicionados antes dos verbos principais. Para as formas negativas e interrogativas os verbos modais não precisam de outros verbos e possuem a mesma forma para todas as pessoas do singular e do plural.

Alguns modais são:

Can, Could

Can e *could* normalmente são usados para expressar habilidades, possibilidades e para pedir ou conceder permissões (em situações mais informais). A forma negativa do modal *can* é *can't* (*cannot*) e a forma negativa do modal *could* é *could not* (*couldn't*).

May

May geralmente é usado para expressar possibilidades, deduções e pedir ou conceder permissões (em situações de uso mais formais). A forma negativa do modal *may* é *may not*.

Must

Em geral, *must* é usado para expressar uma obrigação ou uma dedução. A forma negativa de *must* (*must not* ou *mustn't*) indica uma proibição.

Should

O modal *should* é usado para oferecer conselhos e fazer recomendações. A forma negativa de *should* é *should not* (*shouldn't*).

Conditionals

Conditionals (orações condicionais) indicam o que vai acontecer se uma condição se concretizar. Em língua portuguesa, as orações condicionais estão ligadas ao modo subjuntivo representado pela partícula "se". Em inglês, *conditionals* apresentam situações reais e hipotéticas, representadas mais frequentemente pela conjunção *if*.

If + simple present + simple present: combinação empregada quando nos referimos a uma condição que expressa leis naturais, verdades universais, fatos ou conclusões lógicas.

If + simple present + simple future / can / may / might: combinação se aplica a uma ação ou situação que pode acontecer no futuro.

If + simple present + imperative / should: combinação utilizada para dar ordens, sugestões ou instruções.

As conjunções *whether*, *unless* e *as long as*, entre outras, também podem ser usadas em orações condicionais.

Direct and Indirect Speech

Usamos *direct speech* (discurso direto) para reproduzir o que alguém disse usando exatamente as mesmas palavras, as quais colocamos entre aspas.

Usamos *indirect* ou *reported speech* (discurso indireto) para relatarmos o que uma pessoa disse com nossas próprias palavras.

No discurso indireto normalmente precisamos alterar o tempo verbal, os pronomes e as expressões de tempo e de lugar.

Mudanças de tempos verbais:

Direct Speech	Indirect Speech
Simple Present	Simple Past
Present Continuous	Past Continuous
Present Perfect	Past Perfect
Simple Past	Past Perfect
Will	Would
Can/May	Could/Might
Must	Had to
Imperative	Infinitive

As formas verbais com *could*, *might*, *would* e *should* não sofrem alterações.

Mudanças de expressões de tempo e de lugar:

Direct Speech	Indirect Speech
A week/a month/a year ago	A week/a month/a year before
Last week/month/year	The week/month/year before
Next	The following
Now	Then / at that time
Today	That day
Tomorrow	The next day/the following day
Tonight	That night
Yesterday	The day before/the previous day
Here	There

Na forma interrogativa, para mudarmos do discurso direto para o indireto, usamos a oração na forma afirmativa, fazendo as devidas alterações quanto ao tempo verbal, aos pronomes e às expressões de tempo e lugar. Quando não há uma *wh-question*, usamos a conjunção *if* para reportar o que foi perguntado.

Discourse Markers

Usamos *discourse markers* (marcadores do discurso ou conjunções), também chamados de *linking words*, *cohesive devices* ou *connectors*, para estabelecer relações lógicas entre ideias anteriores e ideias posteriores.

Marcadores do discurso	Relações estabelecidas
And; also; besides; moreover; in addition	Adição
Or; nor; whether; either; neither	Alternativa
As; because; due to; since	Causa
As; like	Comparação
Although; even though; in spite of	Concessão
As long as; except if; if; if not; unless	Condição
Yet; but; however; on the other hand; conversely	Contraste
For instance; for example; particularly; such as	Exemplificação
To; in order to; so as to	Propósito
First; second; next; after that; then; previously; finally	Sequência

Passive Voice

Ao contrário da voz ativa, em que a ênfase está em quem praticou a ação (no sujeito), em geral usamos a voz passiva quando a ação é mais importante do que o agente, quando falamos de uma verdade universal ou quando não é importante mencionar ou não sabemos dizer o que ou quem realizou a ação.

Para formarmos a voz passiva, usamos o verbo *to be* no mesmo tempo verbal do verbo principal da voz ativa, acrescido do particípio passado de tal verbo principal. O sujeito da voz ativa torna-se o objeto da voz passiva e vice-versa.

Para mencionarmos quem ou o que realizou a ação usamos a preposição *by*.

Voz ativa	Voz passiva
Simple Present	are/is + past participle
Present Continuous	is/are + being + past participle
Simple Past	was/were + past participle
Past Continuous	was/were + being + past participle
Future with will	will be + past participle
Future with going to	am/is/are + going to be + past participle
Present Perfect	has/have + been + past participle
Past Perfect	had been + past participle
Modal verbs (can, could, may, might, must, should)	modal verb + be + past participle

Verb Tense Review

Simple Present: usado para fatos, opiniões ou ações rotineiras.

Present Continuous: usado para ações que estão acontecendo no momento da fala.

Present Perfect: usado para ações que aconteceram em algum momento indeterminado do passado e que normalmente têm influência no presente ou continuam até o presente.

Simple Past: usado para ações que ocorreram e tiveram fim em determinado momento do passado.

Past Continuous: usado para ações que estavam em curso no passado.

Past Perfect: usado para ações que aconteceram antes de outras ações no passado.

Simple Future ou *Future with will*: usado para previsões ou decisões tomadas no momento da fala.

Immediate Future ou *Future with going to*: usado para ações que acontecerão em um futuro próximo e que estão planejadas ou previstas.

Phrasal Verbs

Phrasal verbs (verbos preposicionados ou expressões verbais) são verbos combinados com preposições ou partículas adverbiais que complementam ou alteram seus significados. Um mesmo *phrasal verb* pode ter diversos significados diferentes. O estudo dos *phrasal verbs* propicia uma habilidade no uso e na compreensão da língua inglesa de maneira mais natural.

Cognates and False Cognates

Cognates ou *transparent words* (cognatos) são palavras que pertencem a uma mesma família, que têm a mesma origem etimológica e, portanto, apresentam ortografias semelhantes.

False cognates ou *false friends* (falsos cognatos) são palavras que apresentam similaridade com outras mas não possuem ligação semântica alguma com elas.

Word Formation

Em inglês, muitas palavras são formadas pelo acréscimo de uma partícula antes (prefixo) ou depois (sufixo) de suas raízes. A inclusão dos prefixos e sufixos faz com que sejam alteradas as classes das palavras, facilitando assim o estudo e a identificação das categorias gramaticais mesmo que não se conheça os significados de tais palavras. Alguns sufixos são formadores de substantivos (*-er, -or, -ation, -ition, -ment, -ance, -ence* etc.), outros de verbos (*-ify, -ize, -en* etc.), de advérbios (*-ly*) ou de adjetivos (*-ful, -less, -able, -y* etc.). Os prefixos, por outro lado, podem indicar negação (*un-, il-, ir-, -dis* etc.), atitude (*co-, anti-, pro-* etc.), tempo ou sequência (*pre-, post-* etc.), quantidade (*bi-, di-* etc.), entre outras ideias.

LEARNING STRATEGIES

Leitura rápida para exploração geral de textos (*skimming*)

Skimming é uma importante estratégia de leitura que consiste basicamente em fazer uma exploração geral do texto sem se deter, a princípio, em nenhum detalhe específico. Além da leitura rápida dos parágrafos, busca-se por informações como título, datas, autor, de onde o texto foi extraído etc. Ao final dessa exploração, você saberá de que se trata o texto como um todo e, assim, sua leitura e compreensão será muito mais eficiente.

Uso do dicionário bilíngue

Utilizar um dicionário bilíngue o ajudará a elaborar respostas significativas com mais segurança e correção, além de auxiliá-lo na aprendizagem e expansão de vocabulário da língua estrangeira. Um bom dicionário é uma excelente ferramenta de aprendizagem e oferecerá informações importantes, desde os possíveis significados das palavras até as classes gramaticais e áreas do conhecimento às quais podem pertencer.

Identificação de palavras cognatas (palavras transparentes)

As palavras cognatas são aquelas cujas grafias e significados são iguais ou muito semelhantes aos seus correspondentes em língua portuguesa. Por isso, elas são fáceis de ser identificadas e ajudam muito na compreensão geral do texto.

Identificação de falsos cognatos

Os falsos cognatos são palavras que apresentam grafia igual ou semelhante a algumas palavras em língua portuguesa, mas têm significados parcialmente ou totalmente distintos. Identificar os falsos cognatos nos textos o ajudará a evitar equívocos de interpretação.

Prática de inferências

Fazer inferências significa captar o que não está dito de forma explícita no texto. Para inferir algo, é necessário ir além da superfície textual e refletir sobre o que o texto nos diz. Muitas vezes, precisamos associar fatos e informações às nossas experiências de vida para chegarmos a alguma conclusão. A inferência combina conhecimentos prévios e pistas que encontramos nos textos. Ela nos permite extrair novas informações a partir daquilo que está escrito. Assim, as conclusões às quais chegamos ao ler um texto serão fundamentadas e coerentes.

Pesquisa antes da produção escrita

Antes de qualquer produção escrita, pesquise o vocabulário e os elementos linguísticos que você pretende usar em seu texto. Leia e colha informações importantes sobre o assunto. Utilize sempre fontes confiáveis para obter mais conhecimentos sobre o tema a respeito do qual deseja desenvolver seu texto. Escrever bem, tanto na língua materna quanto em língua estrangeira, requer basicamente leitura e prática.

Etapas da produção escrita: revisão e reescrita

A escrita é um processo que deve ser planejado. As etapas de revisão e reescrita são extremamente importantes, pois é por meio delas que é possível refletir sobre o texto e aprimorá-lo, não apenas no sentido de corrigir desvios gramaticais, mas também de deixá-lo mais fluente e coerente para o propósito ao qual se destina.

Uso de referências pronominais

Pergunte-se sempre a que termo do texto determinado pronome se refere. Muitas vezes, o termo ao qual o pronome se refere está posicionado antes dele. Identificar o termo referente facilitará a compreensão dos textos.

Busca por informações específicas em um texto (*scanning*)

Scanning é uma estratégia de leitura que consiste em uma rápida visualização do texto buscando por palavras-chaves, frases ou ideias e informações específicas. Ao utilizarmos essa técnica, sabemos previamente o que estamos procurando. Quando visualizamos um convite, por exemplo, podemos utilizar a estratégia *scanning* para encontrar rapidamente a data, a hora e o local em que ocorrerá o evento.

Leitura prévia de enunciados e propostas em atividades de *listening*

Antes de ouvir textos em inglês ou quaisquer outros idiomas, leia as atividades propostas antes que o professor reproduza o áudio e verifique quais são as informações de que você precisa. Essa estratégia o ajudará a ficar mais atento ao que ouve e ser bem-sucedido nas respostas.

Agrupamento de palavras por campos lexicais

Agrupar as palavras por campos lexicais, ou seja, palavras pertencentes a uma mesma área de conhecimento, pode ser um excelente facilitador no processo de assimilação e ampliação de vocabulário.

Elaboração de glossário pessoal

Tente montar um glossário e criar frases que contextualizem os novos vocábulos. Essa estratégia facilitará seu aprendizado, pois ele será muito mais significativo.

Leitura dos enunciados

Sempre leia os enunciados com bastante atenção, pois, muitas vezes, encontramos neles informações relevantes para realizarmos com sucesso as atividades propostas.

Atenção ao contexto

É muito comum descobrirmos o significado de palavras e expressões desconhecidas apenas por meio da observação atenta do contexto em que elas estão inseridas. Por isso, leia os textos mais de uma vez. Lembre-se também de que uma mesma palavra ou expressão pode ter diferentes sentidos de acordo com o contexto em que é utilizada.

Identificação do gênero textual

Ao ler um texto, procure reconhecer nele características que o ajudem a descobrir a qual gênero textual ele pertence. Essa estratégia pode ajudá-lo na compreensão geral, uma vez que textos do mesmo gênero tendem a ser organizados e estruturados de modo similar.

Busca por detalhes específicos

Algumas perguntas têm como respostas detalhes bem específicos e importantes. Procure ler e reler o texto atentamente, faça associações e selecione essas informações.

Acionamento de conhecimento de mundo

Use seu conhecimento de mundo para refletir sobre assuntos que ainda não sejam de seu total domínio. Troque ideias e esteja aberto para novas descobertas e informações.

Lembre-se também de que, ao fazer previsões, os seus conhecimentos de mundo são acionados. Levante hipóteses, antecipe expectativas e estabeleça conexões com o texto a ser lido. Isso, certamente, facilitará a sua compreensão.

Identificação de prefixos e sufixos

Os prefixos e sufixos são elementos carregados de significado e que formam outras palavras. Por meio deles, alteramos o significado inicial de uma palavra. Identificar e compreender o sentido de prefixos e sufixos lhe dará a oportunidade de ampliar seu vocabulário.

Organização de ideias e conteúdos

Você pode organizar ideias e conteúdos em *mind maps* (mapas mentais). Eles são muito usados na confecção de sumários, na análise de assuntos complexos, na apresentação de informações associadas a um tema central e em muitas outras situações. Os mapas mentais estimulam a criatividade e vão além da memorização de conteúdo, contribuindo para o aprendizado efetivo.

Prática da releitura

Sempre leia os textos mais de uma vez. A cada boa leitura, mais claro ficará o texto. Para tanto, pode ser necessário interromper a leitura em alguns momentos, para refletir sobre o trecho lido. Por isso, volte aos parágrafos anteriores sempre que preciso, até que toda a informação esteja clara para você.

Reconhecimento de marcadores discursivos

Os marcadores discursivos contribuem para a coesão e coerência dos textos escritos e orais. Reconhecê-los vai ajudá-lo a compreender melhor as relações entre as ideias de um texto.

Atenção às datas e imagens

Buscar por datas e observar atentamente imagens que compõem os textos permitem localizar informações específicas com mais rapidez e eficiência.

Aprendizagem por meio de músicas

Ouvir músicas em inglês é um excelente exercício para adquirir vocabulário, conhecer expressões contextualizadas, aprimorar a habilidade de compreensão auditiva e praticar pronúncia. Procure conhecer as letras das músicas de que você mais gosta e aprenda enquanto se diverte.

Aprendizagem por meio de filmes e séries

Sempre que possível, assista a filmes e séries com áudio original em inglês e sem legendas. Além de ser uma forma bastante eficaz de aprender o idioma, você estará em contato com situações reais de comunicação.

Domínio de diversas áreas do conhecimento

Ter bom domínio de diferentes áreas do conhecimento é muito importante, entre outras coisas para compreender melhor os textos. Seus conhecimentos de História e Geografia, por exemplo, podem ajudar muito na melhor compreensão de um texto sobre turismo.

Identificação de números, frações e porcentagens

Procure identificar números, frações e porcentagens em um texto e, em seguida, descubra a que eles se referem. Essa estratégia facilitará a compreensão mais detalhada do que foi lido.

Uso de expressões idiomáticas (*idioms*)

Aprender expressões idiomáticas (*idioms*) é importante porque essas expressões tornam a língua falada mais informal e natural. Lembre-se, porém, de que não devemos traduzi-las ao pé da letra, pois seus significados raramente são literais.

Identificação das figuras de linguagem

Conhecer e identificar as figuras de linguagem presentes nos textos nos permitem interpretá-los de forma mais abrangente, atribuindo novos sentidos às palavras e expressões.

Simulados Enem

Texan teenager's invention can clean up cars' dirty exhaust pipes

Param Jaggi, a 17-year-old high school senior, designed a device called "Algae Mobile". Inside the tubed device are algae that convert carbon dioxide into oxygen through photosynthesis. Drivers would simply need to place the tube into their car's exhaust pipe and let nature run its course. It's taken Param 3 years to develop his idea, with the support of his teachers and peers, into one that was recently recognized by the *EPA with an award for sustainability.

*EPA - Environmental Protection Agency

Nepalese teenager's invention may help make solar panels as cheap as chips

Malin Karki, an 18-year-old teenager, discovered that the melanin that pigments human hair can be used to replace silicon in solar panels. Malin arrived at his idea while reading a book by Stephen Hawking on how to create static energy from hair. Malin's invention has the potential to make solar panels to poor communities across the world.

[…]

Adapted from <teachingforsustainability.com/index.php/2015/04/07/8-teenagers-inventing-the-sustainable-technologies-of-the-future/>. Accessed on May 9, 2016.

1. A instituição educacional *Barack Obama Green Charter High School* elaborou uma lista de alguns jovens de diferentes lugares do mundo que se debruçaram sobre problemas relacionados ao meio ambiente que afetam as comunidades onde vivem. Sobre os projetos dos jovens apresentados no fragmento só não podemos inferir que:

a. a *EPA* está engajada em projetos relacionados à preservação do meio-ambiente.

b. a instituição educacional *Barack Obama Green Charter High School* oferece recursos financeiros para jovens estrangeiros que desenvolvem pesquisas em benefício do meio-ambiente.

c. ambos os garotos têm em comum a proatividade e utilizaram seus conhecimentos com o objetivo de transformar as comunidades em que vivem.

d. um dos mais consagrados físicos da atualidade influenciou positivamente o jovem nepalês em seu invento.

e. ambas as invenções podem beneficiar comunidades em todo o mundo.

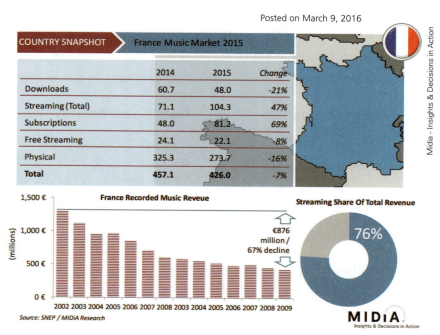

Extracted from <musicindustryblog.wordpress.com/tag/music-sales>. Accessed on May 10, 2016.

2. Os excertos abaixo foram extraídos do blog do analista de mídias e tecnologias especializado na indústria da música, o britânico Mark Mulligan. Selecione a opção que apresenta aqueles que estão diretamente relacionados aos gráficos.

   I. "Perhaps most perplexing though was the fact that ad supported streaming revenue, for both audio and video, declined by 8%."
   II. "Streaming revenues were up an impressive 47% but physical sales fell by 16% and downloads by a staggering 21%."
   III. "Even though the download collapse was seismic, the lost revenue (€12.7 million) was less than half the amount that streaming grew by (€33.2)."
   IV. "We predicted that the continued decline of legacy formats (i.e. the download and the CD) would undo all the positive growth work of streaming resulting in market stagnation/market decline. As the French experience shows us, this reality is already coming to pass."

   a. Apenas I.
   b. II e III.
   c. I e II.
   d. Apenas IV.
   e. III e IV.

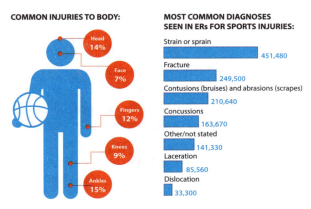

Safe Kids Worldwide, based on hospital ER reports, 2012. Janet Loehrke, USA TODAY

Extracted from <www.usatoday.com/story/news/nation/2013/08/06/injuries-athletes-kids-sports/2612429/>. Accessed on May 11, 2016.

3. A *Safe Kids Worldwide* é uma organização global com atuação em mais de 30 países e dedicada à prevenção de ferimentos em crianças. Leia as proposições abaixo e indique aquela que não corresponde às informações do quadro.

   a. Os ferimentos mais comuns ocorrem pela ordem: nos tornozelos, na cabeça, nos dedos, nos joelhos e no rosto.
   b. Pouco menos de 10% dos ferimentos concentram-se em deslocamentos e lacerações.
   c. Mais de 30% dos ferimentos que ocorrem em crianças durante a prática esportiva são torções.
   d. Pouco mais da metade de crianças esportistas sofre outros tipos de ferimentos não listados no quadro.
   e. Os ferimentos decorrentes da prática esportiva infantil são comuns e podem oferecer riscos sérios à saúde.

#1

Extracted from <www.cartoonstock.com/>.
Accessed on July 5, 2016.

#2

Extracted from <www.cartoonstock.com/>.
Accessed on July 5, 2016.

4. Acerca dos cartuns podemos afirmar que
   a. criticam as perdas que a tecnologia traz para a sociedade, especialmente às crianças.
   b. apenas o cartum 2 aborda a facilidade que as crianças nascidas na era digital têm para lidar com a tecnologia.
   c. ambos mostram que os adultos não conseguem lidar com a rápida evolução da tecnologia tanto quanto os jovens.
   d. ambos abordam de forma crítica e bem-humorada o domínio tecnológico das crianças nascidas na era digital, bem como a decorrente mudança de interesses e de comportamento social e familiar delas.
   e. não há relação temática entre eles, uma vez que o primeiro tem como objetivo principal retratar a chantagem do filho para com o pai e o segundo aborda a confusão cultural da criança causada por influência da tecnologia.

International Day of Women and Girls in Science
February 11

Secretary-General Ban Ki-moon holds an electronic "sensor cane" which earned three female students from the School at Askar Camp in Nablus operated by *UNRWA a "special award in applied electronics" at the Intel International Science and Engineering Fair in San Jose, California.

2016 Theme: "Transforming the World: Parity in Science"

Science and gender equality are both vital for the achievement of the internationally agreed development goals, including the 2030 Agenda for Sustainable Development. Over the past 15 years, the global community has made a lot of effort in inspiring and engaging women and girls in science. Unfortunately, women and girls continued to be excluded from participating fully in science. According to a study conducted in 14 countries, the probability for female students of graduating with a Bachelor's degree, Master's degree and Doctor's degree in science-related field are 18%, 8% and 2% respectively, while the percentages of male students are 37%, 18% and 6%.

In order to achieve full and equal access to and participation in science for women and girls, and further achieve gender equality and the empowerment of women and girls, the United Nations General Assembly adopted resolution A/RES/70/212 (draft A/70/474/Add.2) declaring February 11th as the International Day of Women and Girls in Science.

Commemorating the very first observance of the day, a High-Level Forum is being held on February 11th, 2016 at the United Nations Headquarters by The Royal Academy of Science International Trust (RASIT) and DESA-DSPD. Download the programme and watch the live webcast.

Adapted from <www.un.org/en/events/women-and-girls-in-science-day/>. Accessed on May 9, 2016.

*UNRWA (United Nations Relief and Works Agency for Palestine Refugees)

5. De acordo com o texto, as mulheres e as meninas não têm a oportunidade de participar no setor científico tanto quanto os homens. Embora a comunidade global empenhe esforços, essa desigualdade entre homens e mulheres ainda é significativa.

Selecione o(s) excerto(s) que fundamente(m) essa afirmação.

   I. "Science and gender equality are both vital for the achievement of the internationally agreed development goals, including the 2030 Agenda for Sustainable Development."
   II. "According to a study conducted in 14 countries, the probability for female students of graduating with a Bachelor's degree, Master's degree and Doctor's degree in science-related field are 18%, 8% and 2% respectively, while the percentages of male students are 37%, 18% and 6%."
   III. "[…] the United Nations General Assembly adopted resolution A/RES/70/212 (draft A/70/474/Add.2) declaring February 11th as the International Day of Women and Girls in Science."

a. Apenas o I.
b. I e III.
c. Apenas a II.
d. Todos os excertos.
e. Apenas o III.

Extracted from <cupanabr.blogspot.com.br/2010/11/monicas-gang-comic-strips-historias-em.html>. Accessed on May 11, 2016.

Extracted from <www.juniao.com.br/?attachment_id=815>. Accessed on May 11, 2016.

6. Assinale a única alternativa que **NÃO** está de acordo com os textos.
   a. Tanto a tira quanto a charge convergem em relação à crítica feita à ação devastadora do homem sobre a natureza em nome do progresso.
   b. Uma das características comuns ao gênero textual tira é a presença da comicidade, traço latente na tira de Mauricio de Sousa.
   c. A charge retrata duas situações distintas, porém seus personagens experimentam os mesmos sentimentos: desolação e impotência.
   d. Embora as tiras de Mauricio de Sousa sejam essencialmente ligadas ao universo infanto-juvenil, podemos inferir que o autor, nesse

caso, busca atingir leitores de diferentes faixas etárias, pois o tema é de interesse de todos.
   e. Há indícios na tira de que os pequenos indígenas já tiveram contato com a cultura do homem branco.

"*I have two mommies. I know where the apostrophe goes.*"

Extracted from <www.newyorker.com/cartoons/a15695>. Accessed on May 11, 2016

7. Podemos inferir a partir da leitura do cartum que:
   a. as novas estruturas familiares são comuns e plenamente aceitas no ambiente escolar.
   b. a professora demonstra intolerância em relação ao equívoco linguístico do aluno.
   c. há forte crítica à resistência social em aceitar alunos oriundos das novas concepções de formação familiar.
   d. o aluno demonstra ser uma criança segura que aceita com naturalidade sua estrutura familiar.
   e. a professora é despreparada para lidar com a estrutura familiar do aluno.

[...]

Top 6 facts about child labor
1. A tragedy

More than half of the world's 200 million working children are working under hazardous conditions. Behind every single number is a child denied the right to a childhood – and a normal healthy life.

2. Children pay a high price for cheap labor

Some child laborers work from 6 in the morning until 7 at night for less than 20 cents a day.

3. Producing our everyday products

Most child workers work on farms that produce cocoa, coffee, cotton, rubber, tea, tobacco, and other crops. Studies in Brazil, Kenya, and Mexico have shown that children under 15 make up 25-30 percent of the total labor-force in those commodities.

4. Children in industrial production

About 20 million child workers worldwide are employed in industrial production. Girls and boys produce a range of goods including garments, carpets, toys, matches, brassware, footballs, fireworks, and hand-rolled cigarettes.

5. The end of child labor is within reach

The number of child workers is decreasing, but the rate by which it is happening is slowing. A strong and sustained global movement is needed to provide the extra push towards eliminating child labor.

6. What you can do

Fair trade products are produced without the use of child labor.

Adapted from <www.theworldcounts.com/counters/child_labor_statistics_worldwide/modern_day_child_labor>. Accessed on May 11, 2016.

8. A intenção do texto é fundamentalmente

a. promover a conscientização de que a sociedade pode e deve se mobilizar a fim de erradicar o trabalho infantil.
b. denunciar as péssimas condições de trabalho a que são submetidos os trabalhadores infantis.
c. estimular os países a focar suas ações na educação e em estratégias que promovam o trabalho decente para as famílias.
d. cobrar políticas de apoio, de programas de geração de renda e de qualificação profissional para que as crianças e os adolescentes não precisem trabalhar para complementar a renda familiar.
e. denunciar países como Brasil, Quênia e México, que exploram a mão de obra infantil na produção agrícola.

SONGS ABOUT MOVIES

Inspiration rarely shows up when you're looking for it. Many songwriters have been smacked over the head with an idea while listening to someone else's music or, in this case, watching someone else's movie. The unfolding of a story, the fate of a character, or even a snippet of dialogue has been known to cause a spark of creativity and inspire a song. And don't think the quality of the movie matters. A cheesy romantic comedy can get the wheels turning just as easy as an Oscar-winning drama. A movie you hate can bring out more emotion than one that you love. These are the stories behind some of the many songs inspired by movies.

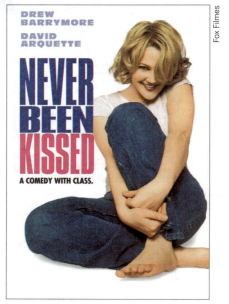

"*One and Only*" by Adele (2011) - Movie: Never Been Kissed. Director: Raja Gosnell, EUA, 1999 (107 min).

I know it ain't easy giving up your heart,
Nobody's perfect,
(I know it ain't easy giving up your heart),
Trust me I've learned it,
Nobody's perfect

Adele isn't fooling anybody. She really likes the Drew Barrymore movie Never Been Kissed, so much so that she wrote a song about it. "One and Only" is actually based on a real-life romance, but part of it was written after she stayed up late watching Barrymore masquerade as a high school student in the romantic comedy.

[...]

Adapted from <www.songfacts.com/blog/writing/songs_about_movies>. Accessed on June 8, 2016.

9. De acordo com o texto, podemos afirmar que

a. a cantora e compositora Adele compôs a canção *One and Only* especialmente para a trilha sonora do filme *Never Been Kissed*.

b. o filme *Never Been Kissed* inspirou apenas parte da letra da música *One and Only*, pois ela essencialmente retrata um romance real.
c. Adele se reconheceu no personagem de Barrymore no filme *Never Been Kissed*, uma vez que a própria compositora já havia vivido a mesma situação retratada no longa.
d. a inspiração para a criação das letras de músicas invariavelmente surge a partir das canções de outros compositores e até mesmo de filmes.
e. filmes cujos enredos apresentam aprofundamento psicológico dos personagens e tramas complexas dignas de concorrer a um Oscar são os que mais inspiram compositores.

About Domestic Violence

[…]

– Who Are The Victims And Perpetrators? –

Research shows that the overwhelming majority (about 95%) of adult victims of domestic violence are women. Although the "norm" of domestic violence relationships is male perpetrator and female victim, anyone can be a victim of abuse.
[…]

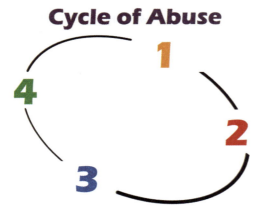

The cycle can occur hundreds of times in an abusive relationship, the total cycle taking anywhere from a few hours, to a year or more to complete. However, the length of the cycle usually diminishes over time so that the "reconciliation" and "calm" stages may disappear.
[…]

Adapted from <ccwrc.org/about-abuse/about-domestic-violence>. Accessed on June 8, 2016.

10. Abaixo estão os textos que compõem o ciclo apresentado. Escolha a opção que os ordene de forma coerente.

I. **Reconciliation**
Abuser apologizes, gives excuses, blames the victim, denies the abuse occurred, or says it wasn't as bad as the victim claims.

II. **Calm**
Incident is "forgotten", no abuse is taking place. The "honeymoon" phase.

III. **Tensions Building**
Tensions increase, breakdown of communication, victim becomes fearful, and feels the need to placate the abuser.

IV. **Incident**
Verbal, emotional, and physical abuse. Anger, blaming, arguing. Threats. Intimidation.

A ordem para que o ciclo ilustre o texto de forma coerente é

a. IV; III; I; II.   c. I; II; IV; III.   e. III; IV; II; I.
b. I; II; III; IV.   d. III; IV; I; II.

Interesting facts about Africa

DECEMBER 4, 2014 BY MANDY MEYER

1. Africa is not a country; it is a continent that consists of 54 countries.
2. Africa is the world's second driest continent (after Australia).
3. The African continent has the second largest population in the world, at about one billion people.
4. The largest religion in Africa is Islam, followed by Christianity.
5. Cairo is the continent's largest city.
6. The world's largest land animal is the African elephant.

7. The fastest land animal in the world, the cheetah, lives in Africa.

8. Africa is home to the world's largest reptile, the Nile crocodile.

9. The gorilla, which can be found in the continent's jungles, is the world's largest primate.

10. Victoria Falls is the largest waterfall in Africa; it is 355 feet high and one mile wide.

11. Mount Kilimanjaro is the highest mountain on the continent.

12. Nigeria is the most populated country with over 145 million people.

[…]

Adapted from <www.africatravelco.com/en/interesting-facts-africa>. Accessed on June 8, 2016.

11. Considere as proposições acerca do texto como V (verdadeiras) ou F (falsas) e assinale a alternativa correta.

I. Considerando que o texto foi veiculado por uma empresa de turismo de aventura por terra, o objetivo dele é apenas expandir os conhecimentos dos turistas sobre o continente africano.

II. A presença recorrente dos superlativos tem por objetivo apresentar a superioridade do continente acerca de diferentes aspectos em relação ao resto do mundo.

III. Dos itens listados, metade deles fazem referência a elementos da natureza africana.

IV. Cinco itens estabelecem comparações considerando como parâmetro o próprio continente africano.

a. F – F – F - V
b. V – V – V - F
c. F – V – F - F
d. V – F – F - V
e. F – V – F – V

Help get control of where your money is going with a personal budget template.

Having control over your money is important, both for your financial well-being and for your peace of mind. Creating a budget with the help of a template can help you feel more in control of your finances and allow you to save more money for your short- or long-term goals.

The following strategies can help you build your personal budget worksheet.

[…]

Creating a budget

Follow these 4 easy steps as you start building your personal budget spreadsheet:

1. Record your daily spending with anything that's handy, whether it's with a pen and paper or an app on your smartphone.

2. Plan for next month's expenses and income so you don't get taken by surprise. Make sure to check in with your significant other before making the list final.

3. Look for ways to spend less. Small savings can add up to a lot of money. Adding one small saving at a time to your budget can surprise you with how much extra money you've accumulated. For example, try shopping at a cheaper grocery store, buying generic brands or experimenting with cooking at home.

4. Find ways to boost your income. Have a hobby or a talent? Anything from handy work to writing or teaching an instrument can be a way to earn extra money. One big bonus about this strategy is that you can make your side business full-time if you ever lose your job. […]

Extracted from <www.bankofamerica.com/deposits/manage/creating-a-budget.go>. Accessed on June 8, 2016.

12. Podemos depreender do texto que sua principal intencionalidade é

a. ensinar de forma didática a economizar dinheiro para que planos futuros sejam concretizados.
b. induzir as pessoas a investir suas economias no Bank of America.
c. dar sugestões para que as pessoas façam pequenas economias no dia a dia.
d. estimular os leitores a buscar por formas alternativas de geração de renda.
e. conscientizar as pessoas de que ter controle sobre o dinheiro garante, além da saúde financeira, bem-estar e, consequentemente, felicidade.

Vestibulares

Universidade Federal de Roraima (UFRR)

Vestibular indígena 2015.2 e 2016.1

1. Read the sentence and complete with the correct alternative.

   Gary told me about his new job. It sounds very _____.
   - a. well.
   - b. interesting.
   - c. dangerously.
   - d. quietly.
   - e. badly.

2. Fill the missing preposition in the following sentence.

   I am very interested _____ football.
   - a. to
   - b. in
   - c. for
   - d. at
   - e. by

3. Complete the question.

   When _____ ? I am not sure. More than 100 years ago.
   - a. was the telephone invented
   - b. has the telephone invented
   - c. did the telephone invent
   - d. was invented the telephone
   - e. the telephone was invented

4. Complete the sentences with the appropriate reflexive pronouns.

   He looked at _____ in the mirror.

   Karen had a good time in Australia. She enjoyed _____.

   I picked up a very hot plate and burnt _____.
   - a. you, his, mine
   - b. him, it, me
   - c. himself, herself, myself
   - d. your, her, my
   - e. us, them, ours

Universidade Federal de São Paulo (Unifesp)

2015

Leia o texto para responder às questões de números 5 a 11.

The Rise of Antibiotic Resistance

By The Editorial Board
May 10, 2014

The World Health Organization has surveyed the growth of antibiotic-resistant germs around the world – the first such survey it has ever conducted – and come up with disturbing findings. In a report issued late last month, the organization found that antimicrobial resistance in bacteria (the main focus of the report), fungi, viruses and parasites is an increasingly serious threat in every part of the world. "A problem so serious that it threatens the achievements of modern medicine," the organization said. "A post-antibiotic era, in which common infections and minor injuries can kill, far from being an apocalyptic fantasy, is instead a very real possibility for the 21st century."

The growth of antibiotic-resistant pathogens means that in ever more cases, standard treatments no longer work, infections are harder or impossible to control, the risk of spreading infections to others is increased, and illnesses and hospital stays are prolonged. All of these drive up the costs of illnesses and the risk of death. The survey sought to determine the scope of the problem by asking countries to submit their most recent surveillance data (114 did so). Unfortunately, the data was glaringly incomplete because few countries track and monitor antibiotic resistance comprehensively, and there is no standard methodology for doing so.

Still, it is clear that major resistance problems have already developed, both for antibiotics that are used routinely and for those deemed "last resort" treatments to cure people when all else has failed. Carbapenem antibiotics, a class of drugs used as a last resort to treat life-threatening infections caused by a common intestinal bacterium, have failed to work in more than half the people treated in some countries. The bacterium is a major cause of hospital-acquired infections such as pneumonia, bloodstream infections, and infections in newborns and intensive-care patients. Similarly, the failure of a last-resort treatment for gonorrhoea has been confirmed in 10 countries, including many with advanced health care systems, such as Australia, Canada, France, Sweden and Britain. And resistance to a class of antibiotics that is routinely used to treat urinary tract infections caused by E. coli is widespread; in some countries the drugs are now ineffective in more than half of the patients treated. This sobering report is intended to kick-start a global campaign to develop tools and standards to track drug resistance, measure its health and economic impact, and design solutions.

The most urgent need is to minimize the overuse of antibiotics in medicine and agriculture, which accelerates the development of resistant strains. In the United States, the Food and Drug Administration (FDA) has issued voluntary guidelines calling on drug companies, animal producers and veterinarians to stop indiscriminately using antibiotics that are important for treating humans on livestock; the drug companies have said they will comply. But the agency, shortsightedly, has appealed a court order requiring it to ban the use of penicillin and two forms of tetracycline by animal producers to promote growth unless they provide proof that it will not promote drug-resistant microbes.

The pharmaceutical industry needs to be encouraged to develop new antibiotics to supplement those that are losing their effectiveness. The Royal Pharmaceutical Society, which represents pharmacists in Britain, called this month for stronger financial incentives. It said that no new class of antibiotics has been discovered since 1987, largely because the financial returns for finding new classes of antibiotics are too low. Unlike lucrative drugs to treat chronic diseases like cancer and cardiovascular ailments, antibiotics are typically taken for a short period of time, and any new drug is apt to be used sparingly and held in reserve to treat patients resistant to existing drugs.

Antibiotics have transformed medicine and saved countless lives over the past seven decades. Now, rampant overuse and the lack of new drugs in the pipeline threaten to undermine their effectiveness.

(www.nytimes.com. Adaptado.)

5. Segundo o texto, um dos objetivos do relatório da Organização Mundial da Saúde é
   a. fazer um levantamento inicial dos principais micro-organismos que causam doenças.
   b. evitar a contaminação de pessoas saudáveis por drogas ineficientes.
   c. identificar os países que não têm dados fidedignos sobre a resistência aos antibióticos.
   d. iniciar uma campanha mundial para desenvolver metodologias para acompanhar a resistência às drogas.
   e. fornecer subsídios à indústria farmacêutica para atualizar as drogas existentes.

6. Segundo o texto, o relatório da Organização Mundial da Saúde
   a. constatou que as infestações por parasitas ainda não têm antídotos eficientes.
   b. concentrou-se no problema das bactérias resistentes aos antibióticos existentes.
   c. utilizou dados detalhados de mais de 114 países para verificar os resultados.
   d. revelou que muitas internações hospitalares são desnecessárias e dispendiosas.
   e. comparou as classes de antibióticos descobertas após 1987 para avaliar sua eficácia.

7. According to the text, last resort antibiotics
   a. have not performed as they should in the case of gonorrhoea in 10 countries.
   b. don't work anymore in all developed countries due to their overuse.
   c. are very expensive and therefore can be taken only in a hospital.
   d. are usually prescribed for intestinal infections by most physicians.
   e. should be replaced by ordinary treatments since they are mostly unsuccessful.

8. According to the fourth paragraph of the text, the Food and Drug Administration
   a. allows the use of growth promoters in agriculture.
   b. convinced animal producers to use only tetracycline to promote animal growth.
   c. banned the use of penicillin and tetracycline by animal producers.
   d. proved that antibiotic use in agriculture doesn't pose any harm.
   e. issued a quite mild guideline to tackle excessive antibiotic use in livestock.

9. No trecho do quarto parágrafo "has appealed a court order requiring it to ban the use of penicillin", o termo em destaque se refere a:
   a. *drug companies.*
   b. *Food and Drug Administration.*
   c. *penicillin.*
   d. *a court order.*
   e. *animal producers.*

10. Segundo o texto, a *Royal Pharmaceutical Society* do Reino Unido afirma que
    a. o câncer e as doenças cardiovasculares também precisam de pesquisas para produzir antibióticos específicos.
    b. há um antibiótico experimental de dose única em testes clínicos desde 1987.

c. o ciclo de tratamento com antibióticos deve ser revisto para que essas drogas sejam viáveis para a indústria farmacêutica.
d. a indústria farmacêutica conseguiu lançar poucos antibióticos alternativos eficientes desde 1987.
e. incentivos financeiros são necessários para o desenvolvimento de novas classes de antibióticos.

11. Segundo o último parágrafo do texto,
a. os antibióticos estão perdendo sua eficácia devido ao seu uso abusivo.
b. daqui a 70 anos os atuais antibióticos estarão todos superados.
c. há diversas pesquisas com novas classes de drogas sendo testadas em animais.
d. muitas pessoas morrerão devido a infecções comuns sem tratamento.
e. o primeiro antibiótico de largo espectro foi criado na década de 70.

Universidade Federal de São Carlos (UFSCAR)

2014

Examine a figura abaixo para responder à questão 12.

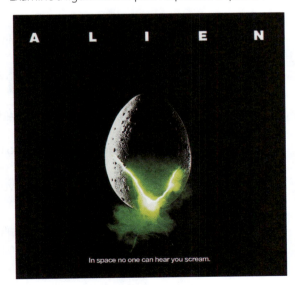

12. A frase do filme pode ser reescrita corretamente, mantendo sentido semelhante, da seguinte maneira:
a. In space no one don't hear you scream.
b. In space no one does not hear you scream.
c. In space no one hear you do not scream.
d. In space no one hears you scream.
e. In space no one hears you doesn't scream.

Universidade Federal de São Carlos (UFSCAR)

2015

Leia a tirinha abaixo para responder às questões 13 e 14.

Disponível em: http://wordpress.com/2012/10/19/while-studying-physics. Acesso em: 13 ago. 2014.

13. O ponto de exclamação do segundo quadrinho permite ao leitor interpretar que o garoto
a. não sabia a resposta à questão da prova, mas se lembrou logo depois.
b. gostou da pergunta da prova porque sabia responder corretamente.
c. lembrou-se de algo que permitiria responder corretamente à pergunta da prova.
d. ficou em dúvida entre duas possíveis respostas, e ao final teve certeza de que escreveu a correta.
e. teve uma ideia de como responder corretamente à pergunta sem saber a resposta.

14. Suponha que, chegando em casa, a mãe do garoto tenha lhe perguntado sobre uma questão da prova e o garoto tenha respondido que:

"it asked to explain Newton's First Law of Motion in _____ own words".

A palavra que completa corretamente o espaço seria:
a. my.
b. his.
c. than.
d. their.
e. it.

Universidade Federal de Santa Maria (UFSM)

2014 – ps2 seriado

Para responder às questões de 15 a 17, leia o texto a seguir.

Shaking up the Salt Myth: The History of Salt

1 The development of human civilization is intricately linked to the pursuit of salt: wild animals wore paths to salt licks, men followed these animals and built settlements near the 5 salt deposits. These settlements became cities and nations. The human obsession with salt has spanned thousands of years of human history, across many different contexts and continents. Nearly every society in existence 10 has some level of salt use not only in their cuisine, but also in their medicine, their politics, their economies, and even their religious practices.

As civilization and agriculture spread, salt 15 became one of the first international commodities of trade, its production was one of the first industries, and a number of the greatest public works were motivated by the need to obtain salt. Salt trade routes 20 traversed the globe, between Africa, Asia, the Middle East, and Europe. Salt was often used as money, and was desperately coveted, hoarded, searched for, traded for, and even fought over.

25 Salt has even made its way into our language as a metaphor for value: hardworking people are known to be "worth their salt", and the most worthy amongst us are known as "the salt of the earth". The root word "sal-" is of 30 Latin origin and refers to salt. Words that have been historically based on humanity's high value for salt include "salubrious", which means "health-living", and "salary", which is derived from the Latin salarium, the money 35 allotted to Roman soldiers for purchases of salt.

"Salus" is the Roman goddess of health and prosperity. Even the word "salad" originated from the Italian salata, as the Romans often 40 ate dishes of assorted raw vegetables with a brined dressing, hence the name which is short for herba salata or "salted vegetables". Nearly four pages of the Oxford English Dictionary are taken up by references to salt, 45 more than any other food. Clearly, the high value placed on salt in many cultures around the world has greatly contributed to the developmental course of human history.

By Chris Kresser, 2012

Disponível em: http://chriskresser.com/shaking-up-the-salt-myth-history-of-salt. Acesso em: 15 set. 2014 (adaptado).

15. Sobre o texto, é INCORRETO afirmar que
   a. a história dos seres humanos e dos animais está ligada ao sal.
   b. as primeiras cidades surgiram próximas a depósitos de sal.
   c. o sal foi um dos primeiros produtos a ser comercializado na humanidade.
   d. historicamente a utilidade do sal tem sido restrita à culinária.
   e. o sal já foi muito valioso, cobiçado e motivo de batalhas.

16. As metáforas "worth their salt" (l.27) e "the salt of the earth" (l.28-29) são usadas para se referir, respectivamente, a
   a. pessoas merecedoras – líderes religiosos.
   b. trabalhadores braçais – trabalhadores voluntários.
   c. pessoas honestas – pessoas ricas.
   d. empregados da indústria do sal – empresários do sal.
   e. pessoas trabalhadoras – pessoas de grande valor.

17. Sobre a palavra sal, considere as informações a seguir.

I – A raíz "sal" vem do Latim e é usada em palavras como "salubre" e "salário", as quais revelam a importância histórica do sal para a humanidade.

II – Está associada à deusa romana da saúde e da prosperidade: "Salus".

III – Ocupa mais espaço do que os demais alimentos no dicionário de língua inglesa Oxford.

Está(ão) correta(s)

a. apenas I.
b. apenas II.
c. apenas II e III.
d. apenas III.
e. I, II, e III

Universidade Estadual de Alagoas (Uneal)

2015 – dia 1

Leia atentamente o Texto 1 e, a seguir, responda às questões de 18 a 29.

TEXTO 1

Are you allergic to mornings?

Are you somebody who can't wake up in the morning? Do you need two cups of coffee before you can start a new day? Do you feel awful when you first wake up? Scientists say it's all because of our genes. How did they find this out? Researchers from the University of Surrey interviewed 500 people. They asked them questions about their lifestyle, for example what time of the day they preferred to do exercise and how difficult they found it to wake up in the morning. Scientists then compared their answers to the people's DNA.

They discovered that we all have a "clock" gene, also called a Period 3 gene. This gene can be long or short. People who have the long gene are usually people who are very good in the morning, but who get tired quite early at night. People who have the short gene are usually people who are more active at night but who have problems waking up early in the morning. How does it help us to know if we have the long or the short gene? Scientists say that, if possible, we should try to change our working hours to fit our "body clock". If you are a "morning person" then you could start work early and finish early. But if you are bad in the mornings, then it might be better to start work in the afternoon and work until late at night. So maybe, instead of nine to five it should be seven to three or twelve to eight.

(Adapted from "New English File – Pre Intermediate", p.93)

18. A frase que melhor resume o conteúdo do Texto 1 é:

a. A grande descoberta dos cientistas da Universidade de Surrey.

b. Você trabalha ou estuda no período que lhe é mais propício?

c. Pesquisas indicam que um gene pode determinar sermos ou não mais predispostos de manhã ou à noite.

d. Cientistas descobrem como podemos ser mais ativos de manhã ou à noite.

e. Pesquisas alertam para problemas em genes naqueles que trocam o dia pela noite no trabalho ou no estudo.

19. Cientistas dizem que, no caso de nos sentirmos mais cansados pela manhã e mais ativos à noite, isso se deve ao fato

a. de que vamos dormir muito tarde da noite.

b. de que consumimos muito estimulante como café, chás ou bebidas alcoólicas antes de dormir.

c. de estarmos altamente estimulados por atividades como televisão, jogos e até esportes.

d. de termos nascido com essa característica, estando geneticamente dispostos a isso.

e. de que tivemos alguma anomalia referente aos nossos genes e que apresentou essa consequência.

20. Os pesquisadores fizeram perguntas sobre

a. o estilo de vida das pessoas, inclusive algumas características específicas.

b. o que conheciam sobre a ciência dos genes e seus determinantes.

c. quais genes exerciam influência sobre eles.

d. qual era o objetivo da Universidade de Surrey.

e. o que sabiam a respeito de suas características genéticas.

21. Eles descobriram que pessoas que possuem um "gene curto"

a. são mais predispostas a estarem mais ativas de manhã e a sentirem-se facilmente cansadas à noite.

b. são mais predispostas a estarem mais ativas à noite e a sentirem-se mais sonolentas de manhã bem cedo.

c. são mais predispostas a estarem ativas do período da manhã até a noite.

d. são menos dispostas durante os períodos da manhã e da noite.

e. são geneticamente doentes e não se encontram ativas nem de manhã, nem à noite.

22. Eles descobriram que pessoas que possuem um "gene longo"

   a. são mais predispostas a estarem mais ativas à noite e a sentirem-se mais sonolentas de manhã bem cedo.
   b. são mais predispostas a estarem ativas do período da manhã até à noite.
   c. são menos dispostas durante os períodos da manhã e da noite.
   d. são geneticamente doentes e não se encontram ativas nem de manhã, nem à noite.
   e. são mais predispostas a estarem mais ativas de manhã e a sentirem-se facilmente cansadas à noite.

23. Saber se o gene é "curto" ou "longo"

   a. poderia permitir à pessoa, na medida do possível, buscar atividades e horários mais propícios às suas características.
   b. não é especificamente útil ainda.
   c. determinaria toda uma opção de atividades para as crianças, de seu nascimento à velhice.
   d. poderia determinar, na medida do possível, as futuras qualificações profissionais de uma criança.
   e. é determinante para a escolha da profissão de uma pessoa, seja no presente ou no futuro.

24. "Body clock" tem sua melhor tradução no português como

   a. corpo relógio.
   b. relógio corporal.
   c. relógio corpóreo.
   d. relógio biológico.
   e. alarme biológico.

25. O gene identificado na pesquisa pode ser LITERALMENTE traduzido por

   a. Gene dos Períodos.
   b. Período dos Genes.
   c. Gene dos 3 Períodos.
   d. 3 Períodos dos Genes.
   e. Gene do Período 3.

26. Na sentença "This gene can be long or short", o verbo modal "can" é utilizado com o sentido de

   a. permissão.
   b. possibilidade.
   c. alternativa.
   d. habilidade.
   e. obrigatoriedade.

27. O Texto 1 apresenta o *Phrasal verb* "wake up" em sua primeira sentença e em algumas outras. Esse *Phrasal verb* é também utilizado corretamente na seguinte frase:

   a. *Did she woke up early the night before?*
   b. *Where has she wake up on her birthday?*
   c. *Are the children still sleeping? Wake them up.*
   d. *He was wakes up by the alarm clock.*
   e. *They wake up later last Sunday.*

28. Na sentença "They asked them questions about their lifestyle", o pronome "them" refere-se

   a. aos cientistas.
   b. aos pesquisadores.
   c. às 500 pessoas.
   d. à universidade.
   e. aos genes.

29. No título do Texto 1, há um cognato-verdadeiro (*allergic* = alérgico). Assinale a alternativa que apresenta um falso-cognato.

   a. *Vocabulary* = vocabulário
   b. *Exam* = exame
   c. *Weather* = tempo
   d. *Actually* = atualmente
   e. *Totally* = totalmente

Leia o Texto 2 e, a seguir, responda às questões de 30 a 33.

TEXTO 2

Children's Health

It's official – British children are getting fatter. According to a survey published in the British Medical Journal in 2001, nearly 16 per cent of two-year-olds are overweight and more than 20 per cent of four-year-olds are overweight. And since 2001, the problem has got worse. The government's latest health survey found that today 30 per cent of all children are overweight.

(Extracted from "New English File/workbook – Pre Intermediate, p.70)

30. O termo "overweight" significa

   a. acima do peso.
   b. abaixo do peso.
   c. no peso certo.
   d. fora do peso.
   e. nessa faixa de peso.

31. Assinale a alternativa que apresenta a ideia principal do Texto 2.

a. As crianças e suas diferentes faixas de peso seguindo sua idade progressiva.
b. O sobrepeso de crianças pequenas a partir de evidências apresentadas em 2001.
c. A saúde das crianças, em especial de algumas, em uma perspectiva do governo.
d. A saúde das crianças maiores em uma perspectiva do Jornal de Medicina de 2001.
e. O estado de saúde oficial das crianças de 2 e 4 anos de idade.

32. O adjetivo "British" remete
   a. à Austrália.
   b. à África do Sul.
   c. aos Estados Unidos da América.
   d. ao País de Gales.
   e. ao Canadá.

33. Em relação à classificação de palavras, os vocábulos "fatter" e "latest" são, respectivamente,
   a. advérbio superlativo e advérbio comparativo.
   b. verbo comparativo e verbo superlativo.
   c. substantivo comparativo e substantivo superlativo.
   d. advérbio comparativo e advérbio superlativo.
   e. adjetivo comparativo e adjetivo superlativo.

Universidade Estadual de Feira de Santana - BA (UEFS)

2013.2

Questões 34 a 38.

Para responder a essas questões, identifique apenas uma única alternativa correta.

Can you spell?

A new website designed to help people with spelling has been unveiled by a British disability charity. Mencap says there is a growing problem with a new generation of people who have been brought up on the computer
5 function which automatically corrects misspelt words. Mencap designed the site because they believe that standards of spelling are falling in Britain, with serious consequences for people's ability to deal with the global downturn. A survey commissioned for the charity revealed
10 that 65% of people were unable to spell the word 'necessary' correctly, and only one-in-five people successfully completed a short spelling test. Despite the results, three-quarters of those questioned thought they were good spellers, and agreed that it was an
15 important skill to have.

Grant Morgan is the Creative Director for the Mencap Spellathon. He says the 'autocorrect' function on computer software is the main culprit for the decline in standards. Mr Morgan says those who can't spell are
20 at an immediate disadvantage in the workplace, and could lose out to competitors if, for example, they misspell words on their CV. In an increasingly tough international market, the problem could damage Britain as a whole. Mencap is holding an online Spellathon championship,
25 where age may well trump youth.

MCMANUS, John. *Can you spell?* Disponível em: <www.bbc.co.uk/worldservice/learningenglish/language/wordsinthenews/2012/05/120604_witn_can_you_spell.shtml>. Acesso em: 13 maio 2013.

34. Fill in the parentheses with T (True) or F (False). Considering the British people questioned, the survey mentioned in the text has shown that
   ( ) despite a decline in ability, most of them are over-confident about spelling success.
   ( ) as the computer autocorrect tool can always be activated, they don't think the spelling ability is all that important.
   ( ) over half of them couldn't spell the word 'necessary' correctly.
   ( ) only one-fifth of them succeeded in doing the spelling test correctly.

According to the text, the correct sequence, from top to bottom, is:
   a. T T T T   c. F T T F   e. T F T T
   b. F T F T   d. T T F F

35. According to Grant Morgan, the computer autocorrect function
   a. is doomed to disappear in the near future.
   b. encourages people to discuss spelling problems.
   c. is to blame for people's decline in the spelling ability.
   d. should be improved in order to adjust to the young generations' needs.

e. is a solution for those people who are good at spelling, especially in the workplace.

36. When the author mentions "the global downturn" (l. 8-9), he refers to
   a. the serious problem of global warming.
   b. the current crisis affecting the world economy.
   c. catastrophic losses involving real state sales.
   d. high expectations concerning the global economy.
   e. drastic cuts in investments in the development of new technologies.

37. About the online Spellathon championship, the author of the text thinks that
   a. older people will probably fail.
   b. age won't play an important role in it.
   c. only old people should take part in it.
   d. young competitors may be at a disadvantage.
   e. youth will certainly have a higher value than experience.

38. Considering language use in the text, it's correct to say:
   a. The verb form "has been unveiled" (l. 2) is in the Active Voice.
   b. The word "misspelt" (l. 5) is a verb form in the Simple Past Tense.
   c. The word "that" (l. 6) is functioning as a relative pronoun.
   d. The word "Despite" (l. 12) is the same as In spite of.
   e. The demonstrative "those" (l. 13) is in the singular form.

Dogged determination

Sometimes scientists seem to be telling us what we already know. Thus a recent study at Britain's University of Portsmouth determined that if you told a dog not to take a piece of meat, then turned out the light
5 so he thought you couldn't see him, he'd likely steal the food anyway.(I once lost half a Thanksgiving turkey like that, but it was no experiment.) What the rigorous testing done with scores of dogs of different breeds at Portsmouth has proved scientifically is that our canine
10 friends really do pay attention to what they're doing – a level of cognition that puts them in a category of intelligence that can begin to be compared with primates. "Dogs show some specialized skills in how they read human communications, says Juliane Kaminski, one of
15 the authors of the Portsmouth study. "This seems to be a direct result of selection pressures during domestication." To put it unscientifically, they've been man's best friend so long, it's in their blood. Kaminski says she doesn't know of any similar studies done on
20 felines. But, then, we already know cats don't really give a damn what humans think.

DICKEY, Christopher. Dogged determination. In "Big Think: Around the world in six ideas." Newsweek, Feb. 25, 2013. p. 9.

39. Fill in the parentheses with T (True) or F (False).

   According to the study mentioned in the text, it's correct to say:
   ( ) Contrary to popular belief, dogs can't see well when it's too dark.
   ( ) As far as food is concerned, dogs can't resist the temptation of getting it, given the opportunity.
   ( ) Dogs are proving to be as smart as primates.
   ( ) Dogs still have a lot of trouble trying to understand what humans want them to do.

   According to the text, the correct sequence, from top to bottom, is:
   a. T F T F   c. F T T F   e. T F T T
   b. F T F T   d. T T F F

40. About cats, the text says that they
   a. have proved to be more obedient than dogs.
   b. can see better in the dark than dogs.
   c. don't care at all about what people think.
   d. are easier to control than dogs.
   e. have difficulty understanding what humans think.

41. Analyze the following:

   "he'd" (l. 5) – "they're" (l. 10) — "man's" (l. 18)

   It's correct to say that the 'd, 're and 's are, respectively,
   a. contraction of "had" – contraction of "were" – contraction of "is".
   b. contraction of "should" – contraction of "are" – "contraction of "was".
   c. contraction of "would" – contraction of "were" – genitive suffix.
   d. contraction of "had" – contraction of "are" – contraction of "is".
   e. contraction of "would" – contraction of "are" – genitive suffix.

42. The word "Thus" (l. 2) expresses
   a. manner.
   b. addition.
   c. condition.
   d. contrast.
   e. choice.

43. The verb "do" (l. 10) is used in the following way:
   a. as a main verb.
   b. for emphasis.
   c. referring back to a previous verb.
   d. helping to form a question.
   e. helping to form a negative.

TEXTO

For the first time, scientists have created human embryos that are genetic copies of living people and used them to make stem cells – a feat that paves the way for treating a range of diseases with personalized body
5 tissues but also ignites fears of human cloning. If replicated in other labs, the methods detailed Wednesday in the journal Cell would allow researchers to fashion human embryonic stem cells that are custom-made for patients with Alzheimer's disease, diabetes and other
10 health problems.
Theoretically capable of reproducing themselves indefinitely, these stem cells could be used to grow replacements for a wide variety of diseased cells – those of the blood, skin, heart, brain, muscles, nerves and
15 more – that would not risk rejection by the patient's immune system.
The report also raises the specter that, with a high-quality donor egg, a bit of skin, some careful tending in a lab and the womb of a willing surrogate, humans
20 have cracked the biological secret to reproducing themselves. That is an objective American scientists have squarely renounced as unethical and scientifically irresponsible. At the same time, most acknowledge that such "reproductive cloning" will one day prove too
25 tempting to resist.
In the hope that other researchers will validate and extend their results, the scientists at Oregon Health & Science University provided an exceptionally detailed account of their techniques. For anyone with a
30 well-equipped fertility lab, the comprehensive guide could also be a useful handbook for cloning a baby. The success of the experiments rekindled debate among bioethicists, who have long anticipated that human cloning would become a reality.

HEALY, Melissa. Disponível em: <www.latimes.com/news/science/sciencenowla-sci-stem-cells-cloning-20130516,0,748507.story>. Acesso em: 13 maio 2013.

44. Fill in the parentheses with T (True) or F (False).

The human embryonic stem cells are considered a major successful achievement because they would
   ( ) be made of the patient's own body tissue.
   ( ) be easily accepted by the patient's immune system.
   ( ) cure all kinds of autoimmune diseases.
   ( ) never be replicated in other labs.

According to the text, the correct sequence, from top to bottom, is:
   a. T T T T
   b. F T F T
   c. F F T T
   d. T T F T
   e. T T F F

45. The word "feat" (l. 3) conveys the idea of something
   a. tough.
   b. awful.
   c. negligible.
   d. impressive.
   e. mysterious.

46. Fill in the blanks with suitable interrogative words. (Wh-questions)

   I. _____ have scientists worked with human embryonic stem cells? This is the first time.
   II. _____ is likely to profit from human embryonic stem cells? Patients with Alzheimer and diabetes, for example.
   III. _____ cells could be replaced by human embryonic stem cells? Those of the blood, skin, heart, and others.
   IV. _____ do humans need to start reproducing themselves? Among other things, a high-quality donor egg, a bit of skin and the womb of a surrogate mother.

According to the text, the correct sequence, from top to bottom, is:
   a. Where / Whose / How old / What
   b. How often / Who / Which / What
   c. What / Which / How many / Who
   d. When / Whom / What / How often
   e. How often / What / How many / When

47. Considering the possibility of human cloning, the American scientists mentioned in the text
    a. are all against it.
    b. can't wait to try it.
    c. intend to do it soon.
    d. don't think it will ever happen.
    e. don't think it's an unacceptable practice.

48. The text says that anyone who could afford a well-equipped laboratory would be able to clone a baby by
    a. just having a team of qualified scientists.
    b. avoiding the mistakes made in previous attempts.
    c. following the detailed instructions given by the scientists.
    d. registering at the Oregon Health & Science University Laboratory.
    e. attending special classes on how to use the new methodology.

49. According to the text, bioethicists
    a. refuse to discuss the issue of human cloning.
    b. avoid talking about the new experiments with stem cells.
    c. have never considered the possibility of human cloning.
    d. started saying that human cloning would happen long before the recent discovery.
    e. are quite sure that the experiments with human embryonic stem cells will end in failure.

50. The only alternative without a pair of opposites is:
    a. "first" (l. 1) – last
    b. "living" (l. 2) – dead
    c. "allow" (l. 7) – encourage
    d. "capable" (l. 11) – unable
    e. "careful" (l. 18) – careless

51. Considering language use in the text, it's correct to say:
    a. The pronoun "them" (l. 3) refers to "people" (l. 2).
    b. The modal "could" (l. 12) expresses possibility.
    c. The word "themselves" (l. 21) is in the singular form.
    d. The word "too" (l. 24) can be replaced by "also" without any change of meaning.
    e. The word "exceptionally" (l. 28) is functioning as an adjective.

DEAR DIARY... Disponível em: <www.cartoonstock.com/directory/w/water_pollution.asp>. Acesso em: 13 maio 2013.

52. In this cartoon, the man on the raft is feeling
    a. sad.   d. hopeful.
    b. tired.   e. stressed.
    c. down.

53. From what the man says, one can infer that he
    a. can already see land.
    b. realizes that he's taking the wrong route.
    c. regrets seeing so much trash on the sea.
    d. doesn't feel like getting back to civilization.
    e. is thrilled because he knows that, where there's pollution, man is nearby.

Universidade Regional do Cariri (Urca)
2016.1

Questions 54 to 56

TEXT

Changing Landscape

Changing temperatures are causing vegetation shifts and conservation challenges. Rising temperatures and changing patterns of rain and snow are forcing trees and plants around the world to move toward polar regions and up mountain slopes.

These vegetation shifts will undermine much of the work the conservation community has accomplished to date, with the potential to permanently change the face of Conservancy preserves, local land trusts, and even our national parks.

In the tundra, thawing permafrost will allow shrubs and trees to take root. In the Great Plains of the United States, grasslands will likely become forests. And New England's fiery fall foliage will eventually fade as maple and beech forests shift north toward cooler temperatures.

As plant communities try to adjust to the changing climate by moving toward cooler areas, the animals that depend on them will be forced to move. Development and other barriers may block the migration of both plants and animals.

Some species and communities such as polar bears and alpine meadows may be left without any remaining viable habitat, putting much of our treasured wildlife at risk.

http://www.nature.org/ourinitiatives/urgentissues/
globalwarmingclimatechange/threatsimpacts/changinglandscapes.xml.
Acessed on October 26, 2015.

54. The words <u>rising</u>, <u>changing</u> and <u>forcing</u> (first paragraph) function, respectively, as

a. adjective – adjective – verb.
b. adjective – adjective – noun.
c. noun – noun – verb.
d. verb – verb – adjective.
e. adjective – noun verb.

55. The pronoun <u>them</u> (fourth paragraph) refers to

a. animals.
b. plant communities.
c. other barriers.
d. plants and animals.
e. cooler areas.

56. After reading the text, one can conclude that

a. polar bears will never be affected by the climate changes because the regions where they live won't suffer with the temperature.
b. animals and plants may migrate from one place to another in order to survive the climate changing.
c. although we are suffering with climate changing, it is quite easy to protect and preserve the vegetation with technology.
d. plants are strong enough to survive the climate changes without being extinct.
e. the human beings are the only ones to be blamed for the climate change.

Universidade do Estado do Rio Grande do Norte (Uern)

2015

Read the text to answer the questions 57, 58 and 59.

What is Ebola?

Ebola is a viral illness of which the initial symptoms can include a sudden fever, intense weakness, muscle pain and a sore throat. And that is just the beginning: subsequent stages are vomiting, diarrhoea and – in some cases – both internal and external bleeding.

Healthcare workers are at risk if they treat patients without taking the right precautions to avoid infection. People are infectious as long as their blood and secretions contain the virus – in some cases, up to seven weeks after they recover.

The virus was first discovered in the Democratic Republic of Congo in 1976 since when it has mostly affected countries further east, such as Uganda and Sudan. From Nzerekore, a remote area of south-eastern Guinea, the virus spread to the capital, Conakry, and neighbouring Liberia and Sierra Leone.

There have been 20 cases of Ebola being imported by someone travelling from a country of widespread transmission to Nigeria, with eight confirmed deaths.

A nurse in Spain became the first person to contract the deadly virus outside of West Africa, after treating two Spanish missionaries who had eventually died of Ebola in Madrid.

Ebola is spread through close physical contact with infected people. This is a problem for many in the West African countries currently affected by the outbreak, as practices around religion and death involve close physical contact.

The ritual preparation of bodies for burial involves washing, touching and kissing. Those with the highest status in society are often charged with washing and preparing the body. For a woman this can include braiding the hair, and for a man shaving the head.

If a person has died from Ebola, their body will have a very high viral load. Bleeding is a usual symptom of the disease prior to death. Those who handle the body and come into contact with the blood or other body fluids are at greatest risk of catching the disease.

Adapted from http://www.bbc.com/news/world-africa-26835233.

How Ebola virus spreads

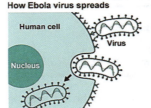
1 Ebola virus fuses with cells lining respiratory tract, eyes or body cavities

2 The virus's genetic contents are released into the cell

3 This genetic material takes over cell machinery to replicate itself

4 New copies of the virus are produced and released back into system

57. Even if you have recovered from the infection

a. your body cannot be handled.
b. you would still have the virus.
c. you might have felt symptoms.
d. cell machinery works perfectly.

58. The item in which the <u>gerund</u> form was used as a noun is:
   a. Those who handle the body are at greatest risk of catching the disease.
   b. Those with the highest social status are charged with preparing the body.
   c. The ritual preparation of bodies for burial involves washing, and kissing.
   d. They treat patients without taking the right precautions to avoid infection.

59. The first step the virus takes is to
   a. reach the cell's nucleus to replicate.
   b. copy the healthy cell genetic material.
   c. merge with some organ's coating cells.
   d. invade the cells' with viral lining tissue.

Use the following image and its text to answer questions 60 and 61.

"Use a large font on your resumé.
It makes your accomplishments look bigger."

(Disponível em: http://www.oregonlive.com/comics-kingdom/?feature_id=Spiderman/.)

60. It is possible to say the character on the right will be
   a. advising on good behavior.
   b. looking for a work position.
   c. handing in a research paper.
   d. finishing some school work.

61. The word <u>it</u> refers back to
   a. use.
   b. font.
   c. resumé.
   d. accomplishments.

Escola Superior de Ciências da Saúde – Brasília (ESCS)
2014

This text refers to questions from 62 through 65.
A New Test And Treatment For Alzheimer's Disease
1 Alzheimer's disease is a deadly neurodegenerative disorder and there's no cure for it. However, scientists appear to have found a compound that could be used to develop a drug
4 for treating patients with Alzheimer's, Parkinson's, Huntington's and other disorders.
As you might know, when a brain cell is hijacked by
7 a virus, the result is the building up of viral proteins. The cells defend by stopping almost all protein production to make sure that the virus doesn't spread.
10 The same defense mechanism is started by many neurodegenerative disorders which involve the production of "faulty" proteins. But the cells shut down the production of
13 proteins for so long that they die due to hunger. This mechanism can lead to the death of neurons throughout the brain, resulting in movement or memory problems or can even
16 be fatal depending on the disorder.
The compound that was used by the scientists prevented the defense mechanisms from being activated, so
19 there was no neurodegeneration. When the compound was used on mice, it prevented all neuron death from prion disease.
Of course, more research is required on the compound
22 before a drug can be developed for use on humans, but this certainly seems to be a good start.
According to Prof. Roger Morris, from King's College London,
25 "This finding, I suspect, will be judged by history as a turning point in the search for medicines to control and prevent Alzheimer's disease".

Adapted from: <www.mobilemag.com>.

62. The main purpose of the article is
   a. to establish a relationship between Alzheimer's disease and other disorders, such as Parkinson's and Huntington's diseases.
   b. to explain what happens when patients suffer from disorders such as Alzheimer's disease.
   c. to reveal that research has found a promising technique which could help with Alzheimer's treatment.
   d. to announce that a new cure for Alzheimer's disease has been discovered.

63. According to the text, it is correct to state that
   a. of the three diseases mentioned, the only one with no cure is Alzheimer's.
   b. brain cells reaction to virus will not lead to neurodegeneration.
   c. the mice used in the experiment were cured from Alzheimer's disease.
   d. Prof. Roger Morris led the team of researchers from the King's College in London.

64. The meaning of "however" (l.2) is equivalent to
   a. "and".
   b. "so".
   c. "for".
   d. "but".

65. Choose which of the options below is the best

equivalent to the excerpt "scientists appear to have found a compound that could be used to develop a drug for treating patients" (l.2-4).

a. scientists seem to have discovered a compound that may be used to develop a drug for treating patients.
b. scientists have found a compound that will be used to develop a drug for treating patients.
c. scientists should have discovered a compound that might be used to develop a drug for treating patients.
d. scientists have probably found a compound that must be used to develop a drug for treating patients.

66. The word "they" in the excerpt "But the cells shut down the production of proteins for so long that they die due to hunger." (l.12-13) refers to
    a. "proteins" (l.13).
    b. "cells" (l.12).
    c. "'faulty' proteins" (l.12).
    d. "neurodegenerative disorders" (l.11).

Universidade Estadual de Minas Gerais (UEMG)
2016

The Red Planet

Mars is a small rocky body once thought to be very Earthlike. Like the other terrestrial planets - Mercury, Venus, and Earth - its surface has been changed by volcanism, impacts from other bodies, movements of its crust, and atmospheric effects such as dust storms. It has polar ice caps that grow and recede with the change of seasons; areas of layered soils near the Martian poles suggest that the planet's climate has changed more than once, perhaps caused by a regular change in the planet's orbit.

Martian tectonism, the formation and change of a planet's crust, differs from Earth's. Where Earth tectonics involve sliding plates that grind against each other or spread apart in the seafloors, Martian tectonics seem to be vertical, with hot lava pushing upwards through the crust to the surface.

Periodically, great dust storms engulf the entire planet. The effects of these storms are dramatic, including giant dunes, wind streaks, and wind-carved features.

Scientists believe that 3.5 billion years ago, Mars experienced the largest known floods in the solar system. This water may even have pooled into lakes or shallow oceans. But where did the ancient flood water come from, how long did it last, and where did it go?

At present, Mars is too cold and its atmosphere is too thin to allow liquid water to exist at the surface for long. There's water ice close to the surface and more water frozen in the polar ice caps, but the quantity of water required to carve Mars's great channels and flood plains is not evident on – or near – the surface today. Images from NASA's Mars Global Surveyor spacecraft suggest that underground reserves of water may break through the surface as springs. The answers may lie deep beneath Mars's red soil.

Unraveling the story of water on Mars is important to unlocking its past climate history, which will help us understand the evolution of all planets, including our own. Water is also believed to be a central ingredient for the initiation of life; the evidence of past or present water on Mars is expected to hold clues about past or present life on Mars, as well as the potential for life elsewhere in the universe. And, before humans can safely go to Mars, we need to know much more about the planet's environment, including the availability of resources such as water.

Mars has some remarkable geological characteristics, including the largest volcanic mountain in the solar system, Olympus Mons; volcanoes in the northern Tharsis region that are so huge they deform the planet's roundness; and a gigantic equatorial rift valley, the Valles Marineris. This canyon system stretches a distance equivalent to the distance from New York to Los Angeles; Arizona's Grand Canyon could easily fit into one of the side canyons of this great chasm.

Mars also has two small moons, Phobos and Deimos. Although no one knows how they formed, they may be asteroids snared by Mars's gravity.

http://science.nationalgeographic.com/science/space/solar-system/mars-article/Text courtesy NASA/JPL-2015.

67. According to the text, what is the CORRECT statement?
    a. Mars and Earth have the same tectonic plates.
    b. Mars and Earth are red planets.
    c. Mars and Earth support the human race.
    d. Mars and Earth have water.

68. Choose and mark the CORRECT statement.
    a. Mars is home to both the highest mountain and the deepest longest valley in the solar system.
    b. Mars experienced the least known floods in the solar system.
    c. Mars does not belong to the solar system.
    d. Mars has two big moons that could not fit into Arizona's Grand Canyon.

69. In the 1st paragraph its refers to
    a. the planets.   c. Earth.
    b. Mars.   d. none of them.

70. In the sentence "Mars has some remarkable geological characteristics, including the largest volcanic mountain in the solar system," each pair of the underlined words are grammatically classified as

a. adverb and adjective.
b. adjective and noun.
c. noun and adjective.
d. noun and adverb.

71. In the sentence "Arizona's Grand Canyon could easily fit into one of the side canyons of this great chasm", the word chasm means

a. closure.
b. union.
c. abysm.
d. juncture.

72. The synonym of the word engulf in the 3rd paragraph is

a. uncover.
b. develop.
c. swallow up.
d. come up.

Universidade do Estado do Rio de Janeiro (Uerj)

2016_1

images1.fanpop.com

73. Besides being funny, comics often expresses criticism. The comic strip criticizes men's incapacity to take the following action:

a. fight what baffles them.
b. confront what fools them.
c. resist what alienates them.
d. avoid what confuses them.

74. Consider the visual representation of the tiger in the comic strip.

The effect of closeness between the tiger and the viewer is obtained in the panel below:

a. 5 b. 6 c. 7 d. 8

75. In the speech balloon of panel 1, the word that appears twice.

The second that fulfils the following cohesive function

a. showing emphasis in speech.
b. refering back to the quotation.
c. pointing to the book in the picture.
d. linking main and subordinate clauses.

76. "And I should know". (panel 4)

Modal verbs can be used to refer to a speaker's attitude.

The modal should indicates that Calvin believes his knowledge of the bad quality of the TV show would be characterized as

a. desirable.
b. probable.
c. surprising.
d. mandatory.

77. By establishing links between different parts of a text, one might guess the meaning of an unknown word.

Based on Calvin's evaluation of the show he is watching, the meaning of the word *tripe*, in panel 8, is

a. fun.
b. trash.
c. pastime.
d. program.

Faculdade de Tecnologia do Estado de São Paulo (Fatec)
2015_2

Leia o texto para responder às questões de 78 a 82.

Technology isn't working

The digital revolution has yet to fulfil its promise of higher productivity and better jobs

If there is a technological revolution in progress, rich economies could be forgiven for wishing it would go away. Workers in America, Europe and Japan have been through a difficult few decades. In the 1970s the blistering growth after the second world war vanished in both Europe and America. In the early 1990s Japan joined the slump, entering a prolonged period of economic stagnation. Brief spells of faster growth in intervening years quickly petered out. The rich world is still trying to shake off the effects of the 2008 financial crisis. And now the digital economy, far from pushing up wages across the board in response to higher productivity, is keeping them flat for the mass of workers while extravagantly rewarding the most talented ones.

It seems difficult to square this unhappy experience with the extraordinary technological progress during that period, but the same thing has happened before. Most economic historians reckon there was very little improvement in living standards in Britain in the century after the first Industrial Revolution. And in the early 20th century, as Victorian inventions such as electric lighting came into their own, productivity growth was every bit as slow as it has been in recent decades.

Adapted from http://tinyurl.com/lv6rj7b. Accessed on February 18, 2015.

78. De acordo com o texto, os efeitos da tecnologia notados na América, Europa e Japão

a. foram positivos para a grande maioria dos trabalhadores, considerando o aumento ocorrido em seus salários.
b. foram positivos para a grande maioria dos trabalhadores, considerando a melhora nas condições de segurança no trabalho.
c. ficaram aquém das expectativas em termos de aumento de produtividade, mas foram satisfatórios com relação a melhores empregos.
d. ficaram aquém das expectativas em termos de melhores empregos, mas superaram as expectativas com relação a produtividade.
e. ficaram aquém das expectativas em termos de aumento da produtividade e de melhores empregos.

79. Pelas informações do texto, um dos resultados da economia digital foi

a. melhorar salários de todos os trabalhadores.
b. recompensar os trabalhadores mais talentosos.
c. duplicar os índices de desemprego devido ao uso da tecnologia.
d. triplicar o número de trabalhadores com acesso a computadores.
e. aumentar o nivel de escolaridade da maior parte dos trabalhadores.

80. O termo "the same thing", em destaque no segundo parágrafo, refere-se a

a. *this unhappy experience.*
b. *living standards.*
c. *talented ones.*
d. *workers.*
e. *wages.*

81. De acordo com o segundo parágrafo do texto,

a. a Revolução Industrial proporcionou melhorias significativas nos padrões de vida na Grã-Bretanha.
b. a experiência frustrante com o progresso tecnológico já ocorrera em outros momentos históricos.
c. o desenvolvimento tecnológico, nas últimas décadas, definitivamente não foi muito expressivo.
d. o uso da luz elétrica trouxe aumentos expressivos nos índices de crescimento de produtividade.
e. a Revolução Industrial apresentou efeitos significativos para a melhoria das condições de segurança no trabalho.

82. Assinale a alternativa que apresenta o uso da voz passiva.

a. *Technology isn't working* (título)
b. *rich economies could be forgiven* (1º parágrafo)
c. *after the second world war vanished in both Europe and America* (1º parágrafo)
d. *In the early 1990s Japan joined the slump* (1º parágrafo)
e. *but the same thing has happened before* (2º parágrafo)

Instituto Tecnológico de Aeronáutica (ITA)

2014

As questões de 83 a 85 referem-se ao texto a seguir:

1 Harvard conducted one of the longest and most comprehensive studies of human development – the 75 year old Grant Study – that's reached some fascinating conclusions regarding the recipe for leading a happy life. The sample group was comprised of healthy male Harvard college students who, over the course of their lifetime, agreed to meet with an array of scientists and researchers who measured their psychological, physical 9 and anthropological traits. Though all identities are confidential, it was recently discovered that John F. Kennedy was a sample participant. Following these men through times of war, their careers, parenthood and old age, the Grant Study has amassed an exorbitant amount of data that deeply reflects the human condition. What can be concluded from seven decades of data? It is quite simple actually; warm relationships between parents, spouses, children and friends have the greatest impact on your health and happiness in old age. The study found 19 that 93 percent of the sample group who were thriving at age 65, had a close relationship with a sibling when they were younger. As George Vaillant, the lead director of the study states, it can all be boiled down into five simple words: "Happiness is love. Full stop." (Business Insider.)

Available at http://www.goodnet.org/articles/1055. Accessed on June 10, 2013.

83. A Grant Study, pesquisa realizada pela Universidade de Harvard,
   a. ( ) teve por objetivo investigar o comportamento de pessoas idosas e felizes.
   b. ( ) possibilitou o levantamento gigantesco de dados sobre pesquisadores de Harvard.
   c. ( ) comprovou que John F. Kennedy foi um homem extremamente feliz.
   d. ( ) chama-se the 75 year old Grant Study por ser homenagem à faixa etária analisada.
   e. ( ) comprovou que felicidade na vida adulta está atrelada às relações afetivas ao longo da vida.

84. Assinale a opção cuja reescrita não altera o sentido de: "Though all identities are confidential, it was recently discovered that John F. Kennedy was a sample participant." (linhas 9-11)
   a. ( ) John F. Kennedy was a sample participant, although nobody knew that.
   b. ( ) In spite of being a sample participant, John F. Kennedy's identity was never discovered.
   c. ( ) The study was confidential, thus the participation of John F. Kennedy was never discovered.
   d. ( ) Besides being a confidential study, John F. Kennedy said he used to be a participant.
   e. ( ) In spite of the fact that all identities are kept confidential, it was recently found out that John F. Kennedy was a sample participant.

85. Substituindo os adjetivos *long* e *comprehensive*, respectivamente, por *easy* e *rich* na oração "Harvard conducted one of the longest and most comprehensive studies of human development" (linha 1), teremos:
   a. ( ) the most easy - the richest
   b. ( ) the easiest - the most rich
   c. ( ) the more easy - the richer
   d. ( ) the easiest - the richest
   e. ( ) the most easy - the most rich

Universidade Estadual de Londrina - (UEL-PR)

2014_2

Leia o texto a seguir, que é de uma campanha publicitária da década de 1960, e responda às questões de 86 a 88.

Disponível em: <http://2.bp.blogspot.com/-y9-7Oh0Ppvk/TaHeDmBy6xl/AAAAAAAAj3g/8aLtAo4VV34/s1600/volkswagenwife1.jpg>. Acesso em: 19 maio 2013.

86. O argumento central no qual essa propaganda está baseada é que as mulheres

a. são motoristas inaptas, portanto, mais cedo ou mais tarde, colidirão os automóveis.
b. são dóceis e gentis, gostam de dirigir e, por isso, merecem um carro popular zero quilômetro.
c. preferem um VW, já que o preço das peças é acessível.
d. magoam os homens ao preferirem carros em que as peças são substituíveis.
e. empobrecem os homens ao usarem o carro para fazer compras em *shopping centers.*

87. Sobre o preconceito às mulheres subentendido pelo fragmento do texto na propaganda, considere as afirmativas a seguir. Assinale a alternativa correta.
I. *Your wife isn't limited to fender smashing.*
II. *You can convenient replace anything she uses to stop the car. Even the brakes.*
III. *So when your wife goes window-shopping in a Volkswagen, don´t worry.*
IV. *A gender comes off without dismantling half the car. A new one goes on with just ten bolts.*
a. Somente as afirmativas I e II são corretas.
b. Somente as afirmativas I e IV são corretas.
c. Somente as afirmativas III e IV são corretas.
d. Somente as afirmativas I, II e III são corretas.
e. Somente as afirmativas II, III e IV são corretas.

88. Com base no texto, considere as afirmativas a seguir.
I. A expressão "Sooner or later" e a imagem do VW amassado reforçam a ideia de que, inevitavelmente, o carro será batido.
II. A expressão "drive home" e a imagem do VW amassado traçam um paralelo entre o modo como as mulheres dirigem seus lares e o modo como dirigem seus carros.
III. A palavra "even", na frase "Even the brakes", indica que as mulheres regularmente utilizam os freios para parar o carro.
IV. A frase "Even the brakes" expressa uma ironia em relação à mulher motorista que utiliza tudo para parar o carro, menos a peça que foi destinada para esse fim.

Assinale a alternativa correta.
a. Somente as afirmativas I e II são corretas.
b. Somente as afirmativas I e IV são corretas.
c. Somente as afirmativas III e IV são corretas.
d. Somente as afirmativas I, II e III são corretas.
e. Somente as afirmativas II, III e IV são corretas.

Universidade do Estado de Santa Catarina (Udesc)

2014_2

TEXT 1

The Question

Is it possible that in the future we will live on another planet?
1 It's hard to say whether in the future we will live on another planet. The Earth provides for us the right balance of necessary conditions so that we can live in reasonable comfort without artificial aid. Through advances in technology, we
5 might certainly be able to create an environment in which we could live on almost any other planet (e.g. a space suit is a miniature of such an environment). But whether another planet out in space
harbors conditions similar enough to earth that we would
10 need little or no "artificial environment" is unknown. We might think that such another planet ought to exist, but it doesn't mean that it necessarily does.
The role of science is to take us from what we think might be true to what really is true and possible. In order for us to
15 live on another planet, we must first find other planets (this is an active field of research that astronomers are now making great progress in), determine whether they are suitable for us, and then travel to them. All of these require significant advances in our knowledge and technology.
20 This is not to say that it is beyond our capabilities, but rather to consider what would need to be done to do it.
It is a question worth pondering, and by thinking about it we can certainly learn many exciting things along the way.
I hope this helps, Jim Lochner for Imagine the Universe!

The Answer: www.imagine.gsfc.nasa.gov.
Acessed on March 24, 2014.

Answer the questions below according to Text 1.

89. All the underlined words represent
a. ( ) auxiliary to the future.
b. ( ) statement words.
c. ( ) deduction only.
d. ( ) prepositions and conjunctions.
e. ( ) modal verbs.

90. The text says that
a. ( ) there might be a possibility of living in another planet with conditions to hold our life due to advanced technologies.
b. ( ) there must be another planet out there to embrace human life sometime in the current year.
c. ( ) no other planet is able to have us there, ever.
d. ( ) we ought not to create technology to live in another planet.
e. ( ) it is possible to live in another planet nowadays.

91. The words "beyond" (l. 20) and "enough" (l. 9) mean, consecutively
    a. ( ) further and not sufficient.
    b. ( ) within and superior.
    c. ( ) yonder and sufficient.
    d. ( ) against and better.
    e. ( ) opposite and sufficient.

92. The right sentence to substitute the one in bold (l. 20) is:
    a. ( ) It's a difficult question.
    b. ( ) We cannot answer this.
    c. ( ) It's beyond imagination.
    d. ( ) Thinking about this is out of question.
    e. ( ) It's something to think over.

Faculdade Católica do Tocantins (Facto)
2016

Leia o texto a seguir e responda às questões 93 e 94.

A recent survey of crime statistics shows that we are all more likely to be burgled now than 20 years ago and the police advise everyone to take a few simple precautions to protect their homes.

The first fact is that burglars and other intruders prefer easy opportunities, like a house which is very obviously empty. This is much less of a challenge than an occupied house, and one which is well-protected. A burglar will wonder if it is worth the bother.

There are some general tips on how to avoid your home becoming another crime statistic. Avoid leaving signs that your house is empty. When you have to go out, leave at least one light on as well as a radio or television, and do not leave any curtains wide open. The sight of your latest music centre or computer is enough to tempt any burglar.

Never leave a spare key in a convenient hiding place. The first place a burglar will look is under the doormat or in a flower pot and even somewhere more 'imaginative' could soon be uncovered by the intruder. It is much safer to leave a key with a neighbour you can trust. But if your house is in a quiet, desolate area be aware that this will be a burglar's dream, so deter any potential criminal from approaching your house by fitting security lights to the outside of your house.

But what could happen if, in spite of the aforementioned precautions, a burglar or intruder has decided to target your home? Windows are usually the first point of entry for many intruders. Downstairs windows provide easy access while upstairs windows can be reached with a ladder or by climbing up the drainpipe. Before going to bed you should double-check that all windows and shutters are locked. No matter how small your windows may be, it is surprising what a narrow gap a determined burglar can manage to get through. For extra security, fit window locks to the inside of the window.

What about entry via doors? Your back door and patio doors, which are easily forced open, should have top quality security locks fitted. Even though this is expensive it will be money well spent. Install a burglar alarm if you can afford it as another line of defence against intruders.

A sobering fact is that not all intruders have to break and enter into a property. Why go to the trouble of breaking in if you can just knock and be invited in? Beware of bogus officials or workmen and, particularly if you are elderly, fit a chain and an eye hole so you can scrutinise callers at your leisure. When you do have callers never let anybody into your home unless you are absolutely sure they are genuine. Ask to see an identity card, for example.

If you are in the frightening position of waking in the middle of the night and think you can hear an intruder, then on no account should you approach the intruder. Far better to telephone the police and wait for help.

93. According to the writer, we should
    a. ( ) avoid leaving our house empty.
    b. ( ) only go out when we have to.
    c. ( ) always keep the curtains closed.
    d. ( ) give the impression that our house is occupied when we go out.
    e. ( ) hide the keys under the door mat.

94. According to the writer, window locks, security locks and burglar alarms
    a. ( ) cost a lot of money but are worth it.
    b. ( ) are good value for money.
    c. ( ) are luxury items.
    d. ( ) are absolutely essential items.
    e. ( ) are not efficient nowadays.

Leia a tirinha a seguir e responda às questões 95 e 96.

95. De acordo com a tirinha, por que Mônica se irritou com o dentista?
    a. ( ) Porque ela não consegue abrir a boca.
    b. ( ) Porque o dente não para de doer.
    c. ( ) Porque o dentista não acha necessário ela abrir a boca.
    d. ( ) Porque o dentista machucou sua boca.
    e. ( ) Porque o dentista não se importou com as queixas dela.

96. O verbo "have" na frase dita pela personagem na tirinha acima indica
  a. ( ) necessidade.
  b. ( ) proibição.
  c. ( ) obrigação.
  d. ( ) certeza.
  e. ( ) ordem.

97. Escolha a alternativa que completa corretamente a frase a seguir:

"If I _____ a more reliable car, I _____ to Spain rather than fly."

  a. ( ) would have – would drive
  b. ( ) had – had driven
  c. ( ) had – would drive
  d. ( ) would have had – would drive
  e. ( ) had – will drive

Faculdade de Ceres (Faceres)
2014_1

Use the comic strip below to answer questions 98 to 101.

Calvin and Hobbes

Disponível em: http://reallifebh.com/aprenda-ingles-com-tirinhas-calvin-e-haroldo

98. According to the comic strip, in which degree is the adjective expressed in "At five tons, he is the largest land mammal"?
  a. Comparative of superiority
  b. Progressive
  c. Comparative of equality
  d. Superlative
  e. Infinitive

99. The verbal tense in "His deafening call shatters the early morning tranquility" is
  a. present simple.
  b. present perfect.
  c. present continuous.
  d. past perfect.
  e. past continuous.

100. "Calvin the elephant wanders the African plain" means
  a. Calvin the elephant explores the African plain.
  b. Calvin the elephant needs the African plain.
  c. Calvin the elephant is in the African plain.
  d. Calvin the elephant looks at the African plain.
  e. Calvin the elephant roams the African plain.

101. The words *land* in "land mammal" and *early-morning* in "early-morning tranquility" are
  a. adjectives.
  b. verbs.
  c. adverbs.
  d. nouns.
  e. subjects.

Faculdade de Ceres (Faceres)
2014_2

Use the comic strip below to answer questions 102-105.

Callous – Convincing Patients to Continue their Medication

Disponível em: http://www.comicsenglish.com/comics/tag/callous-2.

102. According to the comic strip, in which degree is the adjective expressed in "In the long run, your medical bills will be more expensive"?

a. Superlative
b. Progressive
c. Comparative of equality
d. Comparative of superiority
e. Infinitive

103. The conditional statement in "If you don't comply with your maintenance medication your symptoms may recur" is

   a. first conditional. It refers to predictive conditional sentences.
   b. third conditional. This is used to refer to hypothetical, counterfactual situations in the past.
   c. second conditional. The condition expressed is known to be false or is presented as unlikely.
   d. zero conditional. It expresses the idea that a universally known fact is being described.
   e. mixed conditional. It refers to a mixture of the second and third conditionals.

104. "If you don't comply with your maintenance medication" means:

   a. If you don't obey the request of the doctor.
   b. If you obey the request of the doctor.
   c. If you maintain the medication.
   d. If you don't stop the medication.
   e. If you stop medication.

105. The words *may* in "your symptoms may recur" and *will* in "your illness will return" are

   a. modal verbs.
   b. verbs.
   c. adverbs.
   d. volitional verbs.
   e. adjectives.

Escola Superior de Propaganda e Marketing (ESPM)

2016_1

Europe's tide of migrant tragedy can be stemmed only in Africa

While the EU argues over those drowning in the Mediterranean, it overlooks the need to work with the sub-Saharan countries from which people are fleeing.

Over 1,800 migrants have died in the Mediterranean since the beginning of 2015.

One day in October 2013, Enrico Letta, the then prime minister of Italy, stood in front of 302 coffins lined up inside a ventilated room on the island of Lampedusa. They contained the bodies of those who had perished at sea, in the biggest migrant disaster Europe had known at that point.

Some of the coffins were very small: they contained the bodies of children. It was a moment of deep reckoning. Letta suddenly realized that Europe's indifference, and its powerlessness, had created a situation where thousands of human lives were put at risk. For Letta, that day marked the starting point of Mare Nostrum, an operation Italy launched to search and rescue migrants attempting the perilous crossing from Africa to Italy.

Letta tells this story in his recent book Andare insieme, andare lontano [Going Together, Going Far], in which he describes his experience as head of the Italian government in 2013-14. He says the migrant crisis became the "gravest issue" he had to deal with as prime minister. But, as Letta points out, doing something about those deaths wasn't just about putting an end to our shame or sense of guilt. It had to do with a certain conception of civic and political duty. Those boat people in the Mediterranean came as a reminder that there were things that simply had to be done: there were moral obligations. But the fact is also that Italy ended up alone in bearing the brunt of the effort.

A lot of **this** came back to the fore in recent weeks, as even worse mass drownings have occurred off the Italian coast. More than 1,800 people have died in the Mediterranean since the beginning of the year. European ministers have scrambled to produce a list of possible measures, ranging from mandatory national quotas for refugees to the military targeting of trafficking networks in Libya, the country that acts as the biggest launchpad for migrants.

The deeper problem is that only the downstream aspect of the migrant tragedy is being addressed. The issues at the other end – where these migrants come from, and why – have hardly been studied in depth, or with strategic solutions in mind. There has been much focus on the resources for rescue operations, on the situation in Libya, its traffickers and its boats, and on how many asylum seekers will be taken in by European countries. But just as Letta wrote in his book, there is a much larger issue at play here, and one that no one seems quite ready to confront: the question of why millions of people decide to uproot themselves from Africa in search of a better life in Europe.

Concentrating on Syrian war refugees, many of whom now arrive in Europe via other routes, misses a bigger story: the largest group of people crossing the Mediterranean to get to Europe this year were those from sub-Saharan Africa. One Rome-based European official went as far as claiming that "90% to 95% of migrants" who arrived on Italian shores in recent months had come from countries in western and sub-Saharan Africa such as Senegal, Mali or Ivory Coast.

These are not necessarily war refugees, but often young men fleeing poverty, unemployment, repression and corrupt political regimes. They are aware of the risk posed by the potentially deadly crossing of the Med, but willing to take it in the hope of reaching a more affluent part of the world and building a future there. Sub-Saharan Africa is a demographic time bomb waiting to happen: according to some estimates, its population will double by 2050.

Neither the EU nor its member states have engaged in a comprehensive dialogue with these African countries about the causes of migration. It is not just that development aid has shrunk in recent years. It is that African governments haven't even been asked hard questions about the trafficking networks taking root in their countries – Niger banning people-smuggling is so far an honorable exception. Not to mention the money trail: if the business of trafficking humans across the Sahara and the Mediterranean brings in hundreds of millions of dollars annually, surely that pile of money is not hiding under a mattress somewhere in Libya.

Tracking the money, possibly into tax havens, may be more efficient than destroying fishermen's boats. All these questions are pending. To tackle the migration problem, a more far-reaching European approach is needed, not just rescue operations and emotional appeals, however necessary. The geographical dimension of African migration hasn't yet sunk into our minds. Yet how we deal with it will determine Europe's future.

Adapted from *The Guardian*, Friday, 15 May 2015.

106. The **main idea** of the text is that
   a. more than a civic and political duty, tackling the migrant crisis is a moral obligation.
   b. people crossing the Mediterranean are running away from war crises.
   c. Italy is alone putting up with the worst of the migrant crisis.
   d. the migration issue has not been properly addressed yet.
   e. several measures have been taken in order to mitigate the deaths in the sea.

107. According to the text, it is **NOT TRUE** that
   a. great efforts have been made to find out why people are fleeing.
   b. Africa is where the migration tide had its roots.
   c. EU is failing to deal with the real causes of the migrant issue.
   d. stopping the drowning, however essential, is just a part of the problem.
   e. smugglers take profitable advantages of the African migration tide.

108. The pronoun **this** (boldfaced in the text), in the sentence "A lot of **this** came back to the fore in recent weeks, (…)", refers to
   a. Letta's story.
   b. The brunt of the effort.
   c. The migrant crisis.
   d. Italy's gravest issue.
   e. People's sense of guilt.

109. In the last paragraph, the sentence "The geographical dimension of African migration hasn't yet sunk into our minds" means that
   a. our minds haven't been able to overlook the geographical dimension of African migration.
   b. the geographical dimension of African migration hasn't yet been thoroughly looked upon.
   c. we haven't been able to withdraw the geographical dimension of African migration from our minds.
   d. the geographical dimension of African migration hasn't yet been concealed.
   e. the geographical dimension of African migration has been thrust into our minds.

Faculdade de Direito de Franca (FDF-SP)
2014

Super typhoon Haiyan slams into Philippines, at least three dead

FRIDAY, 8 NOVEMBER 2013 14:41

IN: HTTP://WWW.DAILYMIRROR.LK/NEWS/WORLD-NEWS/INTERNATIONAL/38404-SUPERTYPHOON-HAIYAN-SLAMS-INTO-PHILIPPINES-AT-LEAST-THREE-DEAD.HTML

1 The strongest typhoon in the world this year and possibly the most powerful ever to hit land battered the Philippines on Friday, forcing more than a million people to flee, cutting power lines and blowing apart houses.

2 Haiyan, a category-5 super typhoon, scoured the northern tip of Cebu Province and headed west towards Boracay island, both of them tourist destinations, after lashing the central islands of Leyte and Samar with 275 kph (170 mph) wind gusts and 5-6 meter (15-19 ft) waves.

3 Three people were killed and seven injured, national disaster agency spokesman Rey Balido told a news briefing at the main army base in Manila. The death toll could rise as reports come in from stricken areas.

4 Power and communications in the three large island provinces of Samar, Leyte and Bohol were almost completely down but the government and telephone service providers promised to restore them within 24 hours.

5 Authorities warned that more than 12 million people were at risk, including residents of Cebu City, which has a population of about 2.5 million, and areas still reeling from a deadly 2011 storm and a 7.2-magnitude quake last month.

6 "The super typhoon likely made landfall with winds near 195 mph. This makes Haiyan the strongest tropical cyclone on record to make landfall," said Jeff Masters, director of meteorology at U.S.-based Weather Underground.

7 Typhoons and cyclones of that magnitude can blow apart storm shelters with the pressure they create, which can suck walls out and blow roofs off buildings. Lionel Dosdosa, an International Organization for Migration coordinator on Bohol island, the epicenter of an October 15 earthquake that killed 222 people and displaced hundreds of thousands, said power was off and streets were deserted. "It's dark and gloomy, alternating between drizzle and heavy rain", he said.

8 About a million people took shelter in 29 provinces, after President Benigno Aquino appealed to people in Haiyan's path to leave vulnerable areas, such as along river banks, coastal villages and mountain slopes.

9 "Our school is now packed with evacuees," an elementary school teacher in Southern Leyte who only gave her name as Feliza told a radio station. Leyte and Southern Leyte are about 630 km (390 miles) southeast of Manila.

NO POWER, PRAYERS

10 Roger Mercado, governor of Southern Leyte province, said no one should underestimate the storm. "It is very powerful," Mercado told DZBB radio. "We lost power and all roads are impassable because of fallen trees. We just have to pray."

11 In Samar province, links with some towns and villages had been cut, officials said.

12 "The whole province has no power," Samar Governor Sharee Tan told Reuters by telephone. Fallen trees, toppled electric poles and other debris blocked roads, she said.

13 Authorities suspended ferry services and fishing and shut 13 airports. Nearly 450 domestic and eight international flights were suspended.

14 Schools, offices and shops in the central Philippines were closed, with hospitals, soldiers and emergency workers preparing for rescue operations. Twenty navy ships and various military aircraft including three C-130 cargo planes and helicopters were on standby.

15 The state weather bureau said Haiyan was expected to move past the Philippines on Saturday and out over the South China Sea, where it could become even stronger and threaten Vietnam or China.

16 The world's strongest recorded typhoon, cyclone or hurricane to make landfall was hurricane Camille in 1969, which hit Mississippi with 305 kph (190 mph) winds, said Weather Underground's Masters.

17 An average of 20 typhoons hit the Philippines every year.

18 Last year, Typhoon Bopha flattened three coastal towns on Mindanao, killed 1,100 people and caused damage estimated at $1.04 billion.

19 Haiyan is the 24th such storm to hit the Philippines this year.

(Additional reporting by Karen Lema and Erik dela Cruz; Editing by Jeremy Laurence and Robert Birsel)

PARTE A – COMPREENSÃO DE LEITURA

Leia o texto na íntegra e responda às questões a seguir, escolhendo uma alternativa correta em cada uma delas.

110. De acordo com o texto, o mais poderoso tufão até hoje registrado ocorreu
a. nas Filipinas.
b. no Vietnam.
c. em Mindanao.
d. nos Estados Unidos.
e. em 29 províncias das Filipinas.

111. Em 2013, o tufão Haiyan que atingiu as Filipinas foi o
a. primeiro.
b. vigésimo.
c. vigésimo quarto.
d. segundo.
e. quadragésimo quarto.

112. No parágrafo 1, nos é dito que o ciclone foi
a. violento.
b. de baixa intensidade.
c. o mais violento em 2013.
d. de média intensidade.
e. o que menos estragos ocasionou.

113. No parágrafo 3, uma base do exército em Manila reportou que houve
a. 10 mortos.
b. 7 mortos e 3 feridos.
c. 10 feridos.
d. 3 mortos e 7 feridos.
e. mais mortos que feridos.

114. De acordo com o parágrafo 5, a cidade de Cebu sofreu um terremoto em
a. 2011.
b. outubro 2013.
c. novembro 2013.
d. dezembro 2011.
e. novembro de 2011.

115. No parágrafo 8, o presidente Benigno Aquino
a. pediu que os habitantes permanecessem nos lugares em que estavam.
b. disse que os habitantes deveriam ficar perto dos rios.
c. ordenou que os habitantes não deixassem as áreas vulneráveis.
d. levou um milhão de pessoas a procurar refúgios.
e. não considerou o fato como importante.

PARTE B – ASPECTOS LINGUÍSTICOS

116. No parágrafo 4, – *Power and communications in the three large island provinces of Samar, Leyte and Bohol were almost completely down but the government and telephone service providers promised to restore **them** within 24 hours.* – a palavra **them** tem como referente
a. Samar, Leyte and Bohol.
b. three large island provinces.
c. the government and telephone service providers.
d. power and communications.
e. 24 hours.

117. No parágrafo 18, – *Last year, Typhoon Bopha **flattened three coastal towns** on Mindanao, killed 1,100 people and caused damage estimated at $1.04 billion.* – a palavra **flattened** significa
a. crushed them.
b. destroyed them partially.
c. made them fly.
d. reached them lightly.
e. buried them.

118. No parágrafo 10, a palavra **impassable** na sentença – *We lost power and all roads are **impassable*** –, significa
a. impossíveis.
b. bloqueadas.
c. transitáveis.
d. esburacadas.
e. destruídas.

119. No parágrafo 2, no trecho – *after **lashing** the central islands of* – o uso do **ing** na palavra *lashing* se justifica por
a. vir após preposição.
b. ser adjunto adnominal.
c. ser substantivo.
d. ser adjetivo.
e. ser advérbio.

Centro Universitário Franciscano - Santa Maria/RS (Unifra)

2015_1

How to learn a foreign language on a budget

You don't need expensive lessons to start – try smartphone apps, foreign TV and radio, online guides and your local library

Kerstin Hammes
Wednesday, 18 February 2015

You don't have to break the bank to enjoy the value of learning another language.

1 While the benefits that come from learning a second language may in theory be priceless, many are put off by visions of shelling out huge amounts on expensive resources, tuition or immersion courses. The good news

5 is that it is actually possible to learn on a budget. Here are a few tips for spending less and learning more:
Start online
Many new language learners now start with smartphone apps like Duolingo and Memrise which are 10 free. These apps start you off with vocabulary and basic sentences in minutes, and their game-like interface is ideal for anyone whose last contact with a foreign language was a terrifying oral school exam. But you should also make sure that you get plenty of natural input 15 in your target language. Tune in to international radio stations on TuneIn Radio. (…)
Where to get materials for free
For real results, a step-by-step course will help you build up skills. If you like online learning, my best tip is 20 to check out whether your target country's international TV or radio channel offers a structured language course. These courses are produced by broadcasting professionals and offer well-designed courses going from beginner to advanced level. They feature multimedia 25 materials and even soap operas from big names like Deutsche Welle, TV5 Monde and Russia Today. If you prefer materials aimed at English native speakers, the BBC's GCSE Revision area Bitesize has some of the most effective online revision aids I have seen for Irish, 30 Welsh, French, Spanish, and German. (…) Don't forget that pen and paper are also cheap and invaluable language learning tools. Use them to keep track of new words, write down new sentences in full and create your own flash cards. (…) It's also a good idea to visit your local 35 library and let them surprise you. Libraries have access to a large inter-library loan network, so they can get hold of most courses you want. They also have huge amounts of travel guides and phrasebooks to keep you inspired.
Share your goal with others
40 The internet has good enough resources to let you achieve a decent level in most languages from the comfort of your home, but for many of us, learning in isolation is difficult and boring. Even if it's scary to walk into a new room of language lovers, leave the house and 45 connect with other learners right from the start. Making just one friend who shares your goal or interest in another language can make the difference between a fad that you drop after 12 weeks and a new habit for life. (…)
Spend only where it pays off
50 If you do decide to take your language learning further, consider investing in small group or one-to-one tuition. When you hire a language teacher, the money you spend should buy you unrivalled personal attention. The accountability that comes with lessons creates a boost of 55 ongoing motivation that is almost impossible to find for free.
Most private tutors will offer you a free or cheap trial lesson. These don't mean there is a hidden obligation to buy. Instead, a good tutor will want to learn as much as 60 possible about you before charging you money. They are all different and what is simple and comfortable for one person might be difficult for the next. (…) Once you get started, it's easy to get past the idea that studying a foreign language comes with a big financial burden. 65 Remember to take your time and think of your new language as something you will be learning for life, not just for the next six months. There is only one way to fail at language learning, and that is to stop completely.

Adapted from http://www.theguardian.com/education/2015/feb/18/learn-foreign-languagebudget-app-online-library.

120. Assinale a alternativa que apresenta a ideia central do texto.
   a. É fundamental investir na aprendizagem de uma língua estrangeira no atual contexto histórico.
   b. É possível aprender uma língua estrangeira, na era da informação, sem que seja necessário fazer grandes investimentos financeiros.
   c. É esperado do usuário que, após fazer uso de recursos digitais disponíveis *online* gratuitamente, contrate um professor particular, a fim de aperfeiçoar o conhecimento já desenvolvido.
   d. É preciso, já no início do processo de aprendizagem de uma língua estrangeira, interagir com pessoas que tenham objetivos semelhantes.
   e. É evidente a mudança de opinião do aprendiz, em relação ao investimento financeiro a ser feito na aprendizagem de uma língua estrangeira, à medida que o processo avança.

121. Na tentativa de responder à questão apresentada no título, o texto apresenta algumas dicas para quem deseja aprender uma língua estrangeira de forma gratuita. Dentre essas dicas, o texto não considera
   a. fazer uso de aplicativos específicos para o ensino e a aprendizagem de línguas.
   b. ter acesso a emissoras de TV e estações de rádio internacionais e, eventualmente, participar de cursos de línguas transmitidos por esses veículos.
   c. interagir com outros aprendizes da língua estrangeira que, pelo fato de demonstrarem objetivos semelhantes, tornam-se aliados no processo de aprendizagem.
   d. fazer buscas de materiais disponíveis na língua estrangeira, tais como guias de viagem e manuais de conversação, em acervos de bibliotecas locais.

e. participar de programas de intercâmbio linguístico, por um período mínimo de seis meses, em países onde a língua estrangeira é falada por nativos.

122. Assinale (V) Verdadeiro ou (F) Falso para as ideias apresentadas nas seguintes sentenças, conforme o conteúdo do texto.

( ) Embora exista atualmente uma diversidade de recursos digitais destinados à aprendizagem de uma língua estrangeira, a interação entre os pares continua sendo a melhor alternativa, se considerados os resultados obtidos.

( ) Independentemente dos recursos ou ferramentas utilizados, aprender uma língua estrangeira é resultado de um processo contínuo, que demanda paciência e, principalmente, investimento financeiro considerável.

( ) A internet oferece uma quantidade significativa de recursos digitais e ferramentas multimídia que possibilitam aos seus usuários atingir níveis suficientes de aprendizagem em relação à determinada língua estrangeira.

( ) Em virtude da diversidade de ferramentas digitais e recursos multimídia existentes na atualidade, considera-se o uso de materiais tradicionais, tais como quadro-negro, giz e livro didático impresso, ineficiente do ponto de vista didático-pedagógico.

( ) É possível aprender uma língua estrangeira fazendo-se uso de diferentes métodos; logo, a única maneira de não obter êxito algum em relação a essa aprendizagem é interrompendo-a completamente.

A sequência correta é
a. F – F – F – V – V.
b. F – F – V – V – V.
c. F – F – V – F – V.
d. V – V – V – F – F.
e. V – V – F – V – F.

123. No trecho "While the benefits that come from learning a second language may in theory be priceless, many are **put off** by visions of shelling out huge amounts on expensive resources, tuition or immersion courses", a expressão sublinhada é sinônimo de

a. *delay.*
b. *encourage.*
c. *understand.*
d. *apologize.*
e. *advance.*

124. While the benefits that come from learning a second language may in theory be priceless, many are put off by visions of shelling out huge amounts on expensive resources, tuition or immersion courses. (l. 1)
But you should **also** make sure that you get plenty of natural input in your target language. (l. 14)
If you like online learning, my best tip is to check out whether your target country's international TV or radio channel offers a structured language course. (l. 19)
They feature multimedia materials and even soap operas from big names **like** Deutsche Welle, TV5 Monde and Russia Today. (l. 25)
Instead, a good tutor will want to learn as much as possible about you before charging you money. (l. 59)
Os conectivos negritados nos excertos acima expressam, respectivamente, a ideia de

a. tempo – adição – condição – causa – condição.
b. tempo – exemplificação – condição – causa – oposição.
c. oposição – exemplificação – concessão – causa – condição.
d. oposição – adição – condição – exemplificação – oposição.
e. oposição – adição – condição – exemplificação – condição.

125. No excerto "Use **them** to keep track of new words, write down new sentences in full and create your own flash cards" (l. 32), o pronome sublinhado refere-se a(à)

a. caneta e papel.
b. ferramentas *online* de aprendizagem.
c. palavras novas.
d. sentenças completas.
e. cartões de jogos educacionais.

Universidade Estadual do Maranhão (Uema)
2014

Text to questions 126 and 127.

This quintessential ready to move in home boasts an upgraded kitchen with granite counter-tops and updated appliances, new floors with baseboards throughout, and a playground protected by a white aluminum fence. Nestled in a wonderfully peaceful neighborhood and situated on a gorgeous preserve, perfect for bird watching in the winter time, **this gem is sure to be a quick sale**. Also located in the exclusive Estates of Pembroke Shores, a security guard gated community.

YEAR BUILT: 1997

SQUARE FEET: 3428

LISTING TYPE: resale

MLSID: A1815560

PROPERTY TYPE: Single Family

AGENT NAME: Filippo Vespa

Disponível em: <http://hollywood-florida.olx.com/blank-iid-534369630>. Acesso em: 23 jun. 2013.

Disponível em: <http://www.bestadsontv.com/ad/63317/Israel-Cancer-Association-Third-Hand-Smoking...> Acesso em: 31 ago. 2014.

126. O texto, pelo seu propósito comunicativo, é

a. um anúncio de uma casa à venda.
b. um anúncio de uma casa para alugar.
c. uma descrição de uma casa recém-construída.
d. um e-mail de agente de vendas para uma construtora.
e. uma reportagem sobre uma casa de um artista famoso em Hollywood-Flórida.

127. O conceito de coesão textual diz respeito a todos os processos de sequencialização que asseguram (ou tornam recuperável) uma ligação linguística significativa entre os elementos que ocorrem na superfície textual, facilitando a compreensão e a produção de sentido. O substantivo que substitui a palavra **gem** na frase: "[…] this gem is sure to be a quick sale" é

a. *gorgeous preserve.*
b. *neighborhood.*
c. *playground.*
d. *kitchen.*
e. *home.*

Universidade Estadual do Maranhão (Uema)

2015

Para responder às questões 128 e 129, analise a peça publicitária de grande circulação nos EUA.

128. Os elementos da imagem acima permitem identificar um/uma

a. propaganda em um ambiente hospitalar.
b. anúncio de marca de sofá.
c. advertência sobre o tabagismo.
d. convite para um evento.
e. cartaz de um ambiente residencial.

129. According to the picture one may infer that the black and white parts of the sofa refer to somebody's

a. kidney.   d. brain.
b. heart.   e. liver.
c. lungs.

Universidade Estadual de Maringá/PR (UEM)

2015_2
TEXT 1

Are athletes good role models?

1 The term *role model* is defined as "a person
2 whose behavior, example, or success is or can be
3 emulated by others, especially younger people"
4 *(Random House Dictionary).*
5 *Athletes* are *role models* whether or not they
6 choose to take on the responsibility, and whether they
7 are good or bad role models. But athlete "hero
8 worship" wasn't always as prevalent as it is today.

9 There was a time when others served as America's role
10 models (civic leaders, clergy, legal and medical
11 experts, etc.). It might be argued that the shift reflects
12 decay in our nation's moral standards.
13 On the other hand, some exceptional athletes have
14 important messages for their fans. For example, former
15 heavyweight boxing champ Lennox Lewis made a
16 significant contribution to youngsters' understanding
17 of appropriate masculine behavior, when he made a
18 public service announcement that "Real men don't hit
19 women." The point is clear: athletes have an incredible
20 opportunity to use their celebrity power to positively
21 influence the next generation.

Disponível em: <https://www.psychologytoday.com>.
Acesso em: 20 out. 2015.

130. According to **text 1**, choose the **correct** alternative(s).
- **01.** Having a role model means that you admire someone to the point of trying to be like them.
- **02.** Role models' lives are criticized by most psychologists who work with teenagers.
- **04.** Athletes become role models as soon as they get incredibly popular.
- **08.** In the past, American people used to admire people such as doctors and lawyers more than athletes.
- **16.** Fame in sports gives athletes the chance of being a good influence for the future generation.

131. Choose the alternative(s) in which the definition for the word(s) given is **correct**.
- **01.** To emulate (line 3, "emulated"): to make someone feel very sad or disappointed.
- **02.** "worship" (line 8): a strong feeling of love or admiration for someone or something.
- **04.** "clergy" (line 10): the priests in the Christian church.
- **08.** "decay" (line 12): gradual destruction of ideas, beliefs etc.
- **16.** "heavyweight boxing champ" (line 15): a boxer who weighs between 59 and 61 kilograms and is not very successful.

Universidade Estadual do Norte do Paraná (Uenp)

2016

Leia o texto a seguir e responda às questões 132 e 133.

Linguistic imperialism: African perspectives

Abstract

Ninety per cent of the population in Africa today speak only African languages (Ngũgĩ wa Thiong'o, 1992. p.27).

Seventy per cent of South Africa's population understand Zulu (Neville Alexander in Bhanot, 1994). There's no such thing as Nigerian English (Achebe, 1992. p.73).

This is a response to a recent article in ELT Journal on aspects of African language policy (Bisong, 1995). Among the points taken up are: research evidence from African scholars; multilingualism and monolingualism; proposed changes in language policy from the Organization for African Unity and in current initiatives in South Africa; the language that literature is written in; bilingual education; and whose interests ELT is serving.

PHILLIPSON, R. *ELT Journal*. Oxford. v.50. Issue 2. 1996. p.160-167. Disponível em: <http://eltj.oxfordjournals.org/content/50/2/160.abstract>. Acesso em: 25 set. 2015.

132. Considere as afirmativas a seguir.
- I. Este texto pode ser classificado como um gênero acadêmico.
- II. O texto trata de imperialismo linguístico na África.
- III. O autor escreve o texto para responder a um artigo publicado no ano anterior, pela mesma revista (ELT Journal).
- IV. De acordo com o texto, 19% da população africana hoje fala apenas línguas africanas.

Assinale a alternativa correta.
- a. Somente as afirmativas I e II são corretas.
- b. Somente as afirmativas I e IV são corretas.
- c. Somente as afirmativas III e IV são corretas.
- d. Somente as afirmativas I, II e III são corretas.
- e. Somente as afirmativas II, III e IV são corretas.

133. Assinale a alternativa correta.
- a. A pesquisa não aborda a relação entre língua e literatura.
- b. A pesquisa não discute multilinguismo e monolinguismo.
- c. A pesquisa não menciona a educação bilíngue.
- d. A pesquisa não propõe mudanças nas políticas linguísticas.
- e. Pode ser inferido que há interesses subjacentes ao ensino de língua inglesa na África.

Same-sex marriage in the United States

In the United States, same-sex marriage has been legal nationwide since June 26, 2015, when the United States Supreme Court ruled in Obergefell v. Hodges that state-level bans on same-sex marriage are unconstitutional. The court ruled that the denial of marriage licenses to same-sex couples and the refusal to recognize those marriages performed in other jurisdictions violates the Due Process and the Equal Protection clauses of the Fourteenth Amendment of the United States Constitution. The ruling overturned a precedent, Baker v. Nelson.

Disponível em: <https://en.wikipedia.org/wiki/Same-sex_marriage_in_the_United_States>. Acesso em: 1º. out. 2015.

134. Assinale a alternativa correta.

a. Em 26 de junho de 2015, a suprema corte dos EUA declarou legal o casamento entre pessoas do mesmo sexo, pois considerou o impedimento uma violação dos direitos do cidadão americano.

b. Em 26 de junho de 2015, a suprema corte dos EUA declarou legal o casamento entre pessoas do mesmo sexo, por considerar a décima quinta emenda da sua Constituição.

c. Em 26 de junho de 2015, a suprema corte dos EUA negou a legalidade de casamento entre pessoas do mesmo sexo, pois considerou essa negação uma defesa dos direitos do cidadão americano.

d. Em 26 de junho de 2015, o casamento entre pessoas do mesmo sexo tornou-se legal apenas em algumas jurisdições.

e. Em 26 de junho de 2015, o casamento entre pessoas do mesmo sexo tornou-se legal em todos os países do mundo.

Leia o texto a seguir.

Who are minorities?

Minorities of concern to MRG (Minority Rights Group International) are disadvantaged ethnic, national, religious, linguistic or cultural groups who are smaller in number than the rest of the population and who may wish to maintain and develop their identity. MRG also works with indigenous peoples. Other groups who may suffer discrimination are of concern to MRG, which condemns discrimination on any ground. However, the specific mission of MRG is to secure the rights of minorities and indigenous peoples around the world and to improve cooperation between communities.

Unesco. *State of the World's Minorities and Indigenous Peoples 2012*. Reino Unido, 2012. Disponível em: <http://www.unesco.org/library/PDF/MRG.pdf>. Acesso em: 21 set. 2015.

135. Assinale a alternativa que não representa as ideias trazidas pelo texto.

a. A palavra "However" é uma conjunção adversativa, que tem por função ligar a sentença e relacionar os sentidos construídos no texto.

b. O Grupo Internacional dos Direitos da Minoria condena a discriminação, entretanto não atua na melhoria da colaboração entre comunidades.

c. O texto trata como minoria etnias, nações, grupos linguísticos ou culturais que estão em desvantagens em relação ao restante da população.

d. Os indígenas estão inseridos nas minorias defendidas pelo grupo.

e. Os trabalhos do Grupo Internacional dos Direitos da Minoria abordam questões de discriminação e necessidade de preservação de identidade das minorias.

Universidade Estadual do Centro-Oeste (Unicentro)

2016

Read the following advertisement.

Adapted from: <www.innovativeads.tumblr.com/bmw-spareparts-spare->. Accessed on: April 1st, 2015.

136. Based on the advertisement, assign T (True) or F (False) to the following statements.

( ) The ad intends to raise awareness of the severe consequences of making use of alcohol and driving.

( ) It is possible to infer that both body parts and car parts are easily replaceable items.

( ) Despite advances in technology, prostheses will never compare to real body parts.

( ) We may conclude that prostheses have developed so much that they look just like real body parts.

( ) The ad implies that, in car crashes, the most frequently injured body parts are the feet and legs.

Choose the alternative that shows, top-down, the correct sequence.

a. T, T, F, T, F
b. T, F, T, F, F
c. T, F, F, T, T
d. F, T, F, F, T
e. F, F, T, T, T

Centro Universitário Christus – Fortaleza-CE (Unichristus)

2016_2 Medicina

Text

The World Health Organization has declared the Zika virus an international public health emergency, prompted by growing concern that it could cause birth defects. As many as four million people could be infected by the end of the year. Officials at the Centers for Disease Control and Prevention have urged pregnant women against travel to about two dozen countries, mostly in the Caribbean and Latin America, where the outbreak is growing.

The infection appears to be linked to the development of unusually small heads and brain damage in newborns. Some pregnant women who have been to these regions should be tested for the infection, the agency said.

The possibility that the Zika virus causes microcephaly – unusually small heads and often damaged brains – emerged only in October, when doctors in northern Brazil noticed a surge in babies with the condition.

It may be that other factors, such as simultaneous infection with other viruses, are contributing to the rise; investigators may even find that Zika virus is not the main cause, although right now circumstantial evidence suggests that it is.

It is not known how common microcephaly has become in Brazil's outbreak. About three million babies are born in Brazil each year. Normally, about 150 cases of microcephaly are reported, and Brazil says it is investigating nearly 4,000 cases. Yet reported cases usually increase when people are alerted to a potential health crisis.

Google Notícias

137. Durante os últimos meses, tivemos inúmeras manchetes alertando as pessoas sobre uma nova doença se espalhando nas Américas, com imagens chocantes das supostas vítimas: bebês nascidos com cabeças menores que o comum. Mulheres grávidas foram aconselhadas a não viajarem para os países infectados, e o mundo começou a se assustar com a ameaça de uma epidemia como a dos filmes de ficção. Com base no artigo da revista *New York Times*, pode-se afirmar que

a. o Zika é um vírus transmitido por um mosquito que se tornou uma epidemia no Brasil e em outras partes das Américas do Norte e Central.

b. um número maior e incomum de pessoas no Brasil tem a Síndrome de Guillain-Barré, uma doença autoimune rara que pode causar paralisia.

c. a epidemia do Zika no Brasil coincide com o aumento no relato de casos de microcefalia, uma deficiência em que o cérebro não se desenvolve normalmente no útero.

d. a principal causa de microcefalia no Brasil está relacionada ao Zika vírus.

e. o feto é muito vulnerável à infecção porque os tecidos do corpo ainda estão em desenvolvimento e trabalhando na formação de órgãos, por isso, se há uma interrupção no processo, isso pode ocasionar más-formações terríveis que se manifestam como defeitos de nascença".

Centro Universitário de Brasília (Uniceub)

2015_1

Test Instruction: answer the questions from 138 to 140 according to Text 1.

Text 1

Multitasking Damages Your Brain And Career, New Studies Suggest
By Travis Bradberry

You've likely heard that multitasking is problematic, but new studies show that it kills your performance and may even damage your brain.

Research conducted at Stanford University found that multitasking is less productive than doing a single thing at a time. The researchers also found that people who are regularly bombarded with several streams of electronic information cannot pay attention, recall information, or switch from one job to another as well as those who complete one task at a time.

A Special Skill?

But what if some people have a special gift for multitasking? The Stanford researchers compared groups of people based on their tendency to multitask and their belief that it helps their performance. They found that heavy multitaskers – those who multitask a lot and feel that **it boosts their performance** – were actually worse at multitasking than those who like to do a single thing at a time. The frequent multitaskers performed worse because they had more trouble organizing their thoughts and filtering out irrelevant information, and they were slower at switching from one task to another. Ouch.

Multitasking reduces your efficiency and performance because your brain can only focus on one thing at a time. When you try to do two things at once, your brain lacks the capacity to perform both tasks successfully.

Multitasking Lowers IQ

Research also shows that, in addition to slowing you down, multitasking lowers your IQ. A study at the University of London found that participants who multitasked during cognitive tasks experienced IQ score declines that were similar to what they'd expect if they had smoked marijuana or stayed up all night. IQ drops of 15 points for multitasking men lowered their scores to the average range of an 8-year-old child.

Adapted from Forbes Magazine.

138. The main purpose of this text is to
a. show that people who are regularly multitaskers are more productive than the others.
b. point out that some people have a special gift for multitasking and higher IQ.
c. warn people about the risks of being a multitasker.
d. prove that multitaskers are good at organizing thoughts.
e. report that the brain has the capacity to perform lots of things at a time.

139. Choose the letter that best defines the phrase it boosts their performance in the passage.
a. it increases their performance.
b. It reduces their performance.
c. It diminishes their performance.
d. It shortens their performance.
e. It harms their performance.

140. Circle the letter of the answer that correctly contains the following sentence into the negative form. When you try to do two things at once, *your brain lacks the capacity to perform both tasks successfully.*

a. your brain do not lack the capacity to perform both tasks successfully.
b. your brain does not lack the capacity to perform both tasks successfully.
c. your brain does not lacks the capacity to perform both tasks successfully.
d. your brain not lacks the capacity to perform both tasks successfully.
e. your brain not lack the capacity to perform both tasks successfully.

Centro Universitário de Patos de Minas (Unipam)

2014_1

Read the song lyrics below and answer question 141.

WAR (Bob Marley)

Until the philosophy which hold one race
Superior and another inferior
Is finally and permanently discredited and abandoned
Everywhere is war, me say war.
That until there are no longer first class
And second class citizens af any nation
Until the color of a man's skin
Is of no more significance than the color of his eyes
Me say war.
That until the basic human rights are equally
Guaranteed to all, without regard to race
Dis a war.
That until that day
The dream of lasting peace, world citizenship
Rule of international morality
Will remain in but a fleeting illusion
To be pursued, but never attained
Now everywhere is war, war.
And until the ignoble and unhappy regimes
That hold our brothers in Angola, in Mozambique,
South Africa sub-human bondage
Have been toppled, utterly destroyed
Well, everywhere is war, me say war.
War in the east, war in the west
War up north, war down south
War, war, rumours of war.
And until that day, the African continent
Will not know peace, we Africans will fight
We find it necessary and we know we shall win
As we are confident in the victory.
Of good over evil, good over evil, good over evil
Good over evil, good over evil, good ever evil

141. The only saying which DOES NOT have the same thematic relation with the one in Bob Marley's lyrics is

a. "When I say it's you I like, I'm talking about that part of you that knows that life is far more than anything you can ever see or hear or touch. That deep part of you that allows you to stand for those things without which humankind cannot survive. Love that conquers hate, peace that rises triumphant over war and justice that proves more powerful than greed."- Fred Rogers.
b. "The day the power of love overrules the love of power, the world will know peace." - Mahatma Gandhi
c. "World peace must develop from inner peace. Peace is not just mere absence of violence. Peace is, I think, the manifestation of human compassion."- Dalai Lama XIV
d. "When one door closes, another opens; but we often look so long and so regretfully upon the closed door that we do not see the one that has opened for us."- Alexander Graham Bell

Centro Universitário de Volta Redonda - RJ (Unifoa)

2016

TEXTO 1

Back to the Future: What will technology really look like?

The date that Michael J Fox travelled to 30 years ago in the classic movie, Back to the Future is finally here. Flying cars and self-tying shoes have yet to be invented – but video calls and fingerprint recognition are common place today.

But what would he find in another 30 year's time? Scientists at MIT Media Lab in Cambridge, Massachusetts, are at the cutting edge of new technologies. What they design today would well become reality tomorrow.

Story from BBC:http://www.bbc.com/news/world-us-canada-34586525 Published: 21 October 2015

142. The passage inquires about

a. past technologies that can be adapted to the future.
b. futuristic technologies that are under progress in the movies today.
c. the future of classic movies in thirty years.
d. flying cars which can be invented nowadays.
e. which technologies designed today that will actually come true.

Faculdade de Ciências Médicas da Paraíba (Lumen FAC)

2015_1 medicina

Look at the picture below and answer:

Source: Water and Sanitation Program. Available at http://www.wsp.org/content/2013-cartoon-calendar.

143. We can say the cartoon's author sounds

a. pleasant.
b. agreeable.
c. sarcastic.
d. friendly.
e. confident.

Universidade Federal do Espírito Santo (Ufes)

Processo Seletivo Vest. 2014 – 2ª fase [dissertativa]

Working with families helps me break down barriers to learning

by Sue Richards-Gray

I started being interested in how people learn way back when I was at secondary school myself, in Wolverhampton. I was lucky enough to find learning easy but I noticed some of my friends struggled. What stops some people from learning? It was a question I was always asking. When I was in the sixth form, I volunteered in a special school and was interested in how you can get people to do more if you build a relationship with them.

Vestibulares 51

I went to university in Cardiff and studied English literature. Then I did a PGCE at what is now Brunel University in London, I trained as a middle school teacher, thinking I could be more creative in a primary school but wanted to retain my subject specialism.

My first job was in a village primary school in Essex called Churchgate, a small community school where most of the children felt safe, confident and had family backing. Then I did voluntary service in Sarawak, Borneo. I taught English in a secondary school. Each class had 50 children, mostly they lived too far away to come in every day, so they would board in very basic accommodation term time. I managed to build up relationships with many of their families, even visiting their homes despite many of them being over eight hours walk away.

When I came home I got offered a job in Wolverhampton teaching what were then known as remedial classes. It was not a happy place, the children were put into that 'sink' class regardless of their specific difficulty or their year group. I taught them maths, English, history, and geography. They didn't want to be there and I'm not sure I did either.

That's when I moved to Elm Court, a special school in south London. I became early years coordinator for children aged five to eight. The children had a wide range of special needs. I was team teaching 14 children, and everything came back to making a difference to the individual; who had a problem learning and how could I help?

I wanted to do further training in understanding children's behaviour and looked at courses and came upon the Caspari Foundation course for teachers and educational psychologists. I had to be in therapy myself and study a baby from newborn to one year and an older child every week of their life for a year. The school supported me, I did it in the evening and weekends and got one afternoon off a week to do the clinical work.

My training and experience changed the way I taught. I was thinking about the whole child and where they were coming from and what their experience was. I became particularly interested in the notion of attachment developed by John Bowlby and ideas of containment. This is basically the idea that if you feel safe you can take risks and learn but if you don't it's hard to learn; you're too busy looking over your shoulder to see what's coming at you. It's the role of a parent to make their child feel safe, but what if parents aren't able to do that?

I've worked a lot with Child and Adolescent Mental Health Services (CAMHS) over the years in schools and realised some families don't like the idea of it because they think it labels them or their child as "mad". They don't turn up to CAMHS appointments which can be miles away. At Elm Court we decided to set up a one stop shop where parents could come into the school for therapy once a month and meet and talk. They could refer themselves or teachers could advise them to come if their children had emotional or social blocks to learning – it was a real success.

Now I work as a therapist with Schools and Family Works. What we do in schools is close to family therapy based on the Marlborough model of multi-family therapy groups which were originally set up to help families with anorexia and schizophrenia - but in an educational setting.

We work with families a group to help children who have blocks to learning. This might be children who are very withdrawn or particularly disruptive. I go into several different schools and work with a member of the senior management team, as well as parents and children from an average of eight families, so it's quite a big group. All the family is welcome but very often it's the mother and the child. We meet once a week for two hours in school. It's structured and it's safe.

As a therapist I listen and observe: is there a power imbalance? Is the child screaming at the parent or vice versa? We base our work on big targets such as we would like to see 'Jenny' functioning in class, or going to bed and getting up on time for school or being able to talk to friends and not hit them. We play structured games. Parents start to be a resource for their children and for each other. I see the therapy as a bridge for families and schools. Teachers don't have time to spend with families in this way to find the space to breathe, to grow. Usually parents are called into school when something extra terrible happens. But to get in there before, when families aren't coping, is very important.

I think families are crucial for learning. That's the conclusion I've reached through my chequered career. A child needs a whole package and a school needs awareness of the whole child – that includes their families – they don't come on their own. If there's damage with the family's relationships that has an effect on the child, and it goes in circles.

I feel most comfortable with my new role because I know that this is really making a difference and that education doesn't exist in a vacuum. I think there's a danger that we separate education too much from real life and that really concerns me. If I'd known all this when I was teaching full time it would have helped me immeasurably.

Adaptado de: RICHARDS-GRAY, Sue. Working with families helps me break down barriers to learning. Disponível:<http://www.theguardian.com/teacher-network/teacher-blog/2013/apr/07/families-learning-barriers-teaching?INTCMP=SRCH>. Acesso em: 5 set. 2013.

ALL THE QUESTIONS IN THIS EXAM MUST BE ANSWERED IN ENGLISH

144. USE YOUR OWN WORDS to answer the following questions according to the text in complete sentences. DO NOT COPY FROM THE TEXT! Answers which are literally transcribed from the text will NOT be considered.

1. What made Sue Richards-Gray decide to study in order to become a middle school teacher?
2. Why was Sue unsuccessful in her job in Wolverhampton?
3. What made Child and Adolescent Mental Health Services (CAMHS) more successful at Elm Court?
4. Which conclusion did Sue reach through her experience as an educator?
5. What has always been Sue's focus throughout her career?

145. Complete the following sentences using the words below taken from the text.

> be in therapy – set up – the role of – stop them from – board in – turn up – build up – regardless of – one stop shop – looking over

1. The kid's parents could never _____ misbehaving.
2. Young people are always eager to _____ their own business.
3. After years of marriage, they managed to _____ a connection with their in-laws.
4. She would make appointments to see a doctor, but would never _____.
5. He accepted the job right away, _____ salary or working conditions.

146. Use your own words so as to complete the conversation between Sue Richards-Gray (S) and an Interviewer (I), while she is applying for a job.

1. (I): _____
   _____?
   (S): I studied English literature at Cardiff University.
2. (I): What kind of experience did you have abroad?
   (S): _____
   _____.
3. (I): Where did you receive your psychology training?
   (S): _____
   _____.
4. (I): _____
   _____?
   (S): Well, I had to do it in the evenings and weekends.
5. (I): _____
   _____?
   (S): I hope to establish a bridge for families and schools.

147. Use your own words so as to complete the following sentences about Sue Richards-Grey.

1. Even though Sue really loves her profession, she _____
   _____
2. Sue thinks parents must come to schools from time to time, otherwise,
   _____
   _____

Vestibulares 53

3. By the time Sue turns 50 years old, she
_____
_____

4. Sue decided that, rather than changing careers, she
_____
_____

5. As long as her school keeps supporting her, Sue
_____
_____

148. Number the sentences below from 1 to 6 in the correct order so as to create a coherent paragraph. The first sentence is already numbered for you.

Educational therapy

( ) This form of therapy offers a wide range of intensive interventions that are designed to remediate learning problems.

( ) The difference between traditional tutoring and educational therapy is dramatic.

( ) The therapy helps the student strengthen the ability to learn.

( ) The student engages in activities that help academics as well as teach processing, focusing, and memory skills.

( ) Such interventions are individualized and unique to the specific learner.

(1) Educational Therapy is a form of therapy used to treat individuals with learning differences, disabilities, and challenges.

Adaptado de: <http://en.wikipedia.org/wiki/Educational_therapy>. Acesso em: 5 set. 2013.

Universidade Federal do Espírito Santo (Ufes)

Processo Seletivo Vest 2015 – 2ª fase [dissertativa]

What makes a language attractive – its sound, national identity or familiarity?

The allure of a language may have more to do with perceptions of that country's status and social values than its actual sound.

(1) Je t'aime, ti amo, te quiero mucho ! Sounds nice, doesn't it? If you swoon over sweet nothings whispered in French, Italian or Spanish, you're not alone. But while learning to speak a language famed for its romance may increase your sex appeal, the reason for your preference of one vernacular over another may have little to do with how the sounds roll off the tip of your tongue.

(2) Polyglot Roman emperor Charles V declared: "I speak Spanish to God, Italian to women, French to men, and German to my horse." While the 16th century ruler's views may still hold true to some today, his unflattering opinion of the latter language is more likely to be influenced not by the power and status of the country at the time than the tone of its speakers.

(3) Sociolinguists believe the attractiveness of a language is determined by how positively we view a particular group of people who share a cultural outlook. According to Dr. Vineeta Chand of the University of Essex, if we have a positive perception of a particular community then we tend to have equally positive views of the language they speak. Language value and attractiveness is, she explains, linked to the prestige of the speaker. In other words, the socioeconomic and mobility advantages the language affords. Chinese, for example, is gaining in popularity because it is seen as an area of economic growth and speaking that particular tonal tongue means better job prospects. Languages spoken by a community that are less economically powerful may not be seen in the same positive light.

(4) Similarly, we value languages that allow us to speak to a wider audience. English, therefore, is seen as more valuable because it gives us the ability to communicate outside of a small regionally defined context, whereas a language that is spoken by a much smaller community, such as Hawaiian, is not seen as important or appealing. "There is nothing in the sound of the language that makes it less or more attractive," insists Chand. "Some sounds are more common across the world but that doesn't link to the specific perceptions we have about French and Italian. The idea that a language is more melodic, romantic, poetic and musical is derived from those communities and regions."

(5) There are, however, specific sounds in many foreign languages that a native English speaker may find alien and therefore harder on the ear. Languages that have different linguistic structures, such as using tones or sounds that are not found in a listener's native tongue, are probably going to sound less enticing. "English speakers are drawn to the melody of a language such as French or Italian," explains Dr. Patti Adank, a lecturer on speech, hearing and phonetic sciences at University College London (UCL). "In comparison, languages such as Thai or Mandarin can sound harsh because they are using tonal distinctions. It sounds very unnatural and unexpected."

(6) In his book *Through the Language Glass: Why the World Looks Different in Other Languages* Israeli linguist Guy Deutscher agrees that if a language includes rarer sounds, it is more likely to be perceived as less attractive to those unfamiliar with it. The same, he writes, applies to unusual sound combinations such as consonant clusters. He cites the combination "lbstv" in "selbstverständlich" – the German word for "obvious" – as an example of how strange phonetics can grate on a foreign ear. Deutscher explains: "Italian, for example, has very few, if any, sounds that are not shared by other European languages, and few consonant clusters, and it is widely considered a beautiful language. This may not be a coincidence."

(7) Despite many people's fascination with the subject, there has been surprisingly little research conducted to explore it further. Chand says the biggest hurdle to understanding why some languages sound more inviting than others is separating subjective opinion from scientific fact. Labelling certain languages as ugly or beautiful is also a dangerous game many linguists are keen not to play.

(8) She says: "We spend a lot of time in linguistics dispelling myths and the notion of hierarchical languages in terms of attractiveness, grammar and rules. There is less research on this because it is opening a can of worms you don't really want to encourage. "There hasn't been any research that I know of that has directly exploited the attractiveness of a language and didn't eventually tie it back to the social evaluation of the speaking community."

Adaptado de: JENKIN, Matthew. *What makes a language attractive – its sound, national identity or familiarity?* Disponível em: <http://www.theguardian.com/education/2014/jul/17/what-makes-a-language-attractive>. Acesso em: 18 set. 2014.

ALL THE QUESTIONS IN THIS EXAM MUST BE ANSWERED IN ENGLISH

149. USE YOUR OWN WORDS to answer the following questions, according to the text, in complete sentences. DO NOT COPY FROM THE TEXT! Answers which are literally transcribed from the text will NOT be considered.

1. What issue is being discussed in this text?
2. In the past, what made a foreign language be viewed as attractive?
3. Why does Dr. Chand think that sound is not determinant in the appeal of a language?
4. What makes one's attraction to a language less likely?
5. What would be the best answer to the question posed in the title?

150. Complete the following sentences using words found in the box below.

> common – increasingly – other – carries – consolidated – across – information – globalized – linguist – corner

1. There may be more native speakers of Chinese, Spanish or Hindi, but it is English they speak when they talk _____ cultures.
2. It is English they teach their children to help them become citizens of an _____ intertwined world.
3. At telephone call centers around the world, the emblem of a _____ workplace, the language spoken is, naturally, English.
4. On the radio, pop music _____ the sounds of English.
5. They go to almost every _____ of the earth.

151. Complete the following sentences taking into account the meaning of the underlined words as they appear in the text.

1. <u>While</u> I fully understand your point of view, _____

2. <u>Despite</u> repeated assurances that the product is safe, _____

3. When your parents are angry with you, they are more <u>likely</u> to _____

4. <u>If</u> a student is too shy to participate in class, _____

5. Although computer games may be extremely <u>enticing</u>, _____

152. Complete the following sentences using the words in parentheses in the correct order.

1. English has become the _____.
   (everybody – language – of – second)
2. All over the world to be educated _____.
   (English – means – know – to)
3. English has invaded the workplace along _____.
   (global – the – economy – with)
4. Swedish companies use English within the workplace, although _____.
   (Sweden – are – they – in)
5. A lot of their business is _____.
   (through – Internet – done – the)

153. Fill in the blanks below with the correct form of the word in parentheses, using one of the following suffixes: -ing, -less, -ful, -ment.

1. Teaching is _____ (MEANING) if students fail to learn.
2. Education will experience some trouble with the _____ (GRAY) of teachers.
3. _____ (USE) as they may sound, these techniques should be tested before implementation.
4. Teaching is a _____ (REWARD) career for many people; however, it can become frustrating when you have difficulty inspiring unmotivated students.
5. The expansion of _____ (ENROLL) will contribute to the crowding of classrooms.

Universidade Federal do Espírito Santo (Ufes)

Processo Seletivo Vest 2016 – 2ª fase [dissertativa]

Learning styles and language learning

Research in the field of Second Language Acquisition shows that students learn in different ways, so what works well for one learner may not be useful for another. Since learning styles seem to be a relatively stable learner characteristic, teachers may not be able to exert as much influence over this learner variable as, perhaps, over motivation. However, it has been recommended that teachers should adapt classroom tasks in order to maximize the potential of individual learners with particular learning styles. It has also been found that it is also possible that learners over time can be encouraged to incorporate approaches to learning they were resisting in the past. The challenge is to successfully design and deliver language instruction relevant to a multiplicity of learning styles.

It is possible that learning style may vary according to individuals, but also there may be stylistic variation according to gender, age, or nationality. This may mean, for instance, that classes with a majority of male students may have a different dominant style from a mainly female class, and may require different types of activities which cater for their needs. The key for teachers in planning instruction is to be aware of the multiple ways students learn best.

During the planning and preparation stage, teachers should include a variety of language learning tasks so as to allow learners with different styles to do well and achieve success. Materials should be selected from a variety of scholarly books, refereed journals, the Internet, magazines and newspapers, videos, documents, and so on, since different students will have different interests, and will respond more or less favorably to different stimuli. Teachers should also remember that one of the most important contributions of the learning styles concept to language teaching is the understanding that there is no one "best" method for every student.

In order to successfully teach language to children and adults of different cultures, ethnicities, and/or nationalities, teachers need to become familiar with various methods for teaching diverse populations and develop a strong knowledge of and empathy for the learners. This knowledge includes the learners' cultures and languages, their personality structures, their learning styles, their identities, and their inner selves.

Only then can adequate and appropriate learning and teaching decisions be made. Therefore, this implies that good methods and good textbooks cannot be simply imported and good language teachers cannot be simply transferred from one cultural context into the next and be expected to be just as successful in the new environment.

It is clear that learning is very influenced by culture. In settings where the teacher–student relationship is characterized by a high index in power distance (Hofstede, 1980), classroom communication, for example, might look very different compared to settings where the power distance index is low. This will influence the special characteristics of what good communication looks like. We must also be aware that this index may change over time. There are many factors that need to be considered in relation to good language learning. These factors include learning attitudes, learning motivation, and values attributed to learning as well as values associated with learning and education in society.

Today we know that culture as well as other learner variables determine whether a language learner has a strong drive to communicate and to learn from communication or not. Culture influences whether learners are inhibited or not, whether and how much they practice and so on.

GRIFFITHS, Carol (Ed.) *Lessons from Good Language Learners.* Cambridge University Press, 2008. p. 137.

ALL THE QUESTIONS IN THIS EXAM MUST BE ANSWERED IN ENGLISH

154. IN YOUR OWN WORDS, answer the questions below, according to the text, in complete sentences. DO NOT COPY FROM THE TEXT! Answers which are transcribed from the text will NOT be considered.
1. Explain the important learner variable discussed in the first part of the text.
2. Why should teachers be aware of the concept of learning styles?
3. A predominance of either male or female students in a class may require special attention on the part of the teacher. Why?
4. Why is it a mistake to think that there is a "best method" that supposedly meets all the students' needs?
5. List two ways in which culture influences language learning.

155. Express your views on education by completing the sentences below.
1. Learning a foreign language can be a pleasant experience. However, _____
_____
_____
_____
2. Teachers need to be well informed about research so as to _____
_____
_____
_____

3. Since each teacher-learner(s) situation is distinct, the teacher _____
_____
_____
_____
_____

4. A foreign language usually exhibits the cultural traits of its community of speakers. Therefore, _____
_____
_____
_____

5. My success as a language student depends on whether _____
_____
_____
_____
_____

156. Decide which gap(s) below need(s) to be completed with a word and which one(s) must be left blank.
For those requiring a word, write it in the gap. For those requiring nothing, mark a cross (X).
1. Researchers failed to understand ____ nature of ____ problem, he argued.
2. As my friend from ____ school said, ____ life is what happens to you while you're busy making other plans.
3. ____ Brazilians are often regarded as friendly and free-spirited, with ____ incredible zest for life.
4. What has been ____ longest war-free period in ____ History?
5. It is now well-known that ____ exercising and ____ sleep are supposed to be very good for your health.

157. Complete the gaps in the sentences below with a form derived from the underlined words.
1. Don't be so <u>anxious</u>. Control your _____!
2. I <u>refused</u> the new position, and my _____ is final.
3. I <u>warned</u> you more than once. I think I gave you enough _____.

4. He was tried by court martial, convicted, and sentenced to death. I was at the _____.

5. Who discovered this? Who made this amazing _____?

158. In the short texts below, people describe situations involving cultural misunderstandings in foreign countries. Fill in the gaps using the cues in parentheses. Write your answers in the numbered blanks at the bottom of the page.

A British colleague invited me to join his friends after work. We **1** (GO) to a pub where he bought me a drink and he suggested a meal in a restaurant. At the end of the meal, I was very surprised to see everyone **2** (TAKE OUT) their wallets to pay the waiter. My friend expected me to pay as well, but I feel it was very mean of him not to pay for me as he invited me. (Kenji, Japan)

I **3** (VISIT) Germany for the first time and I decided to pay my most important customer a visit. She **4** (INVITE) me for quite some time. I decided to take her a beautiful bunch of twelve red roses and her husband a bottle of wine. I gave her the flowers, but she just looked embarrassed. (Douglas, Scotland)

When I was at university in England, my English tutor invited a group of us to her home. I didn't want to make any mistakes, such as **5** (STAY) too late. So when she brought us a drink before we began the meal, I said, 'Thank you for inviting us to your home and for inviting us to dinner. Could you tell me when we can leave?' She laughed and said, 'So, you can't wait **6** (LEAVE)?'. (Lu, China)

I **7** (RECENTLY/ARRIVE) in the USA and don't have many friends yet, so, I was pleased to meet a really nice American in the college cafeteria the other week. We had a long conversation, she told me the story of her life, she showed me photos of her family, and left me her address. The following week I saw her, but although she smiled and said 'Hi!' in a friendly way, she went and sat with other friends. I feel very hurt. **8** (SHE/EXPECT) me to call on her? I feel I need an invitation. (Hana, Lebanon)

I was sitting in a bus in Bristol when an elderly lady got on the bus. It **9** (BE) crowded and there weren't any seats. A middle-aged man said very loudly, **10** (YOU/OFFER) the lady your seat, please?' Why didn't he give her his seat? (Carlos, Spain)

1. _____
2. _____
3. _____
4. _____
5. _____
6. _____
7. _____
8. _____
9. _____
10. _____

Gabarito

Simulados Enem
1. b
2. b
3. d
4. d
5. c
6. b
7. d
8. a
9. b
10. d
11. e
12. a

Vestibulares

Universidade Federal de Roraima (UFRR)

Vestibular indígena 2015.2 e 2016.1

1. b
2. b
3. a
4. c

Universidade Federal de São Paulo (Unifesp)

2015

5. d
6. b
7. a
8. e
9. b
10. e
11. a

Universidade Federal de São Carlos (Ufscar)

2014

12. d

Universidade Federal de São Carlos (Ufscar)

2015

13. e
14. a

Universidade Federal de Santa Maria (UFSM)

2014 – ps2 seriado

15. d
16. e
17. e

Universidade Estadual de Alagoas (Uneal)

2015 – dia 1

18. c
19. d
20. a
21. b
22. e
23. a
24. d
25. e
26. b
27. c
28. c
29. d
30. a
31. b
32. d
33. e

Universidade Estadual de Feira de Santana - BA (UEFS)

2013.2

34. e
35. c
36. b

37. d
38. d
39. c
40. c
41. e
42. a
43. b
44. e
45. d
46. b
47. a
48. c
49. d
50. c
51. b
52. d
53. e

Universidade Regional do Cariri (Urca)

Processo Seletivo 2016.1

54. e
55. b
56. b

Universidade do Estado do Rio Grande do Norte (Uern)

2015

57. b
58. c
59. c
60. b
61. b

Escola Superior de Ciências da Saúde – Brasília (ESCS)

2014

62. c
63. b
64. d
65. a
66. b

Universidade Estadual de Minas Gerais (UEMG)

2016

67. d
68. a
69. b
70. b
71. c
72. c

Universidade do Estado do Rio de Janeiro (Uerj)

2016_1

73. c
74. c
75. b
76. a
77. b

Faculdade de Tecnologia do Estado de São Paulo (Fatec)

2015_2

78. e
79. b
80. a
81. b
82. b

Instituto Tecnológico de Aeronáutica (ITA)

2014

83. e

84. e

85. d

Universidade Estadual de Londrina - PR (UEL)

2014_2

86. a

87. d

88. b

Universidade do Estado de Santa Catarina (Udesc)

2014_1

89. a

90. a

91. c

92. e

Faculdade Católica do Tocantins (Facto)

2016

93. d

94. a

95. c

96. a

97. c

Faculdade de Ceres (Faceres)

2014_1

98. d

99. a

100. e

101. a

Faculdade de Ceres (Faceres)

2014_2

102. d

103. a

104. e

105. a

Escola Superior de Propaganda e Marketing (ESPM)

2016_1

106. d

107. a

108. c

109. b

Faculdade de Direito de Franca (FDF-SP)

2014

110. a

111. c

112. c

113. d

114. b

115. d

116. d

117. a

118. b

119. a

Centro Universitário Franciscano - Santa Maria/RS (Unifra)

2015_1

120. b

121. e

122. c

123. a

124. d

125. a

Universidade Estadual do Maranhão (Uema)

2014

126. a

127. e

Universidade Estadual do Maranhão (Uema)

2015

128. c

129. c

Universidade Estadual de Maringá/PR (UEM)

2015_2

130. 04 + 16 = 20

131. 02 + 04 + 08 = 28

Universidade Estadual do Norte do Paraná (Uenp)

2016

132. d

133. e

134. a

135. b

Universidade Estadual do Centro-Oeste (Unicentro)

2016

136. b

Centro Universitário Christus – Fortaleza-CE (Unichristus)

2016_2 medicina

137. c

Centro Universitário de Brasília (Uniceub)

2015_1

138. c

139. a

140. b

Centro Universitário de Patos de Minas (Unipam)

2014_1

141. d

Centro Universitário de Volta Redonda - RJ (Unifoa)

2016

142. e

Faculdade de Ciências Médicas da Paraíba (Lumen FAC)

2015_1 medicina

143. c

Universidade Federal do Espírito Santo (Ufes)

Processo Seletivo Vest 2014 – 2ª fase [dissertativa]

As bancas elaboradoras esperam obter da maioria dos candidatos respostas como as que seguem. No entanto, para a correção das provas, outras respostas também poderão ser consideradas, desde que corretas.

144.

1. She believed that such training would enable her to be a more creative teacher in her job as a primary school teacher.

2. Because the children had different difficulties and belonged to different year groups.

3. The creation of a space where parents could come when they wanted/needed to discuss their children's problems with their teachers.

4. That the school must have a full understanding of the child, the child's family, and their relationships in order to achieve its goal to educate.

5. She has always been interested in finding out why some people have more difficulty to learn.

145.

1. stop them from

2. set up

3. build up

4. turn up

5. regardless of

146.

1. What field did you specialize in at the university?
2. I taught English in a secondary school in Sarawak, Borneo.
3. At the Caspari Foundation.
4. How did you manage to find time?
5. What do you expect as a therapist?

147.

1. … has already considered the possibility of giving it up.
2. … their children's rate of success decreases.
3. … will have gathered a considerable amount of experience.
4. … would insist in the choice she made.
5. … will go on being a dedicated teacher.

148. (2); (6); (4); (5); (3); (1)

Universidade Federal do
Espírito Santo (Ufes)

Processo Seletivo Vest 2015 – 2ª fase [dissertativa]

As bancas elaboradoras esperam obter da maioria dos candidatos respostas como as que seguem. No entanto, para a correção das provas, outras respostas também poderão ser consideradas, desde que corretas.

149.

1. The reasons why a language may be preferred over another.
2. It was the tone or melody of the language.
3. Because even though some sounds are common to several languages, that is not connected to the perception we have of a certain language.
4. Linguistic structures and sounds that do not exist in the listener's native language.
5. It's the national identity.

150.

1. across
2. increasingly
3. globalized
4. carries
5. corner

151.

1. …I have to disagree with it.
2. …some people reported feeling sick after using it.
3. …ground you!
4. …he/she should be encouraged by the teacher.
5. …they may also be quite addictive.

152.

1. … second language of everybody.
2. … means to know English.
3. … with the global economy.
4. … they are in Sweden.
5. … done through the Internet.

153.

1. meaningless
2. graying
3. useful
4. rewarding
5. enrollment

Universidade Federal do Espírito Santo (Ufes)

Processo Seletivo Vest 2016 – 2ª fase [dissertativa]

A banca elaboradora espera obter da maioria dos candidatos respostas como as que seguem. No entanto, para a correção das provas, outras respostas também poderão ser consideradas, desde que corretas.

154.

1. Learning styles are individual stable characteristics that learners have and that influence/determine their specific ways of learning.

2. Teachers need to be aware of the concept of learning styles in order to take e learners' differences into consideration when teaching; in order tto motivate them, in order to encourage learners s to incorporate approaches to learning that they do not naturally have and in order to give all kinds of learners the chance to achieve success.

3. Because learners are different not only in terms of learning styles, but also as a result of their age, nationality or gender. In the case of male/female classes, the predominance of male learners may mean a different dominant class, compared to a predominantly female group.

4. Because learners are very different and respond differently to *stimuli*, so, the adoption of certain materials and methods does not guarantee the same results for all learners.

5. Two of the following ways: the power-distance between learners and teachers may affect the type of interaction they have; the idea of what good communication is may vary from culture to culture; learners' attitude; learners' motivation; values attributed to learning; values attributed to education.

155.

1. …it also requires effort and, sometimes, involves failure.
2. …incorporate new knowledge to her teaching.
3. …should account for different learning styles.
4. …when we learn a foreign language, we expand our cultural knowledge/perception.
5. …I make an effort to learn.

156.

1. the / the
2. X / X
3. X / an
4. the / X
5. X / X

157.

1. anxiety
2. refusal
3. warning
4. trial
5. discovery

158.

1. went
2. take out
3. was visiting
4. had been inviting
5. staying
6. to leave
7. have recently arrived
8. Does she expect
9. was
10. Would you offer